Klett Lektürehilfen

Aldous Huxley

Brave New World

Interpretationshilfe für Oberstufe und Abitur

von
Horst Mühlmann

Inhaltsangabe der Lektüre als MP3-Download unter www.klett-lerntraining.de. Klicken Sie bei Downloads Lektürehilfen an.

Sie können auch direkt auf die Seite gehen mit:
www.klett-lerntraining.de/main/book-03_12-downloads

Klett Lerntraining

Dr. Horst Mühlmann, Gymnasiallehrer für Englisch und Deutsch in Bonn, in der Lehrerfortbildung tätig.

Die Zitate zum Text des Romans beziehen sich auf die Ausgabe:
Aldous Huxley: Brave New World. Annotations by Rudolph Franklin Rau. Stuttgart: Ernst Klett Sprachen, 2007.
Zur Verifizierung der zahlreichen Zitate aus den Werken Shakespeares kann jede verfügbare Ausgabe herangezogen werden, die über eine Zeilenzählung verfügt. Diese variiert im Allgemeinen nur sehr geringfügig.

Bibliografische Information der Deutschen Nationalbibliothek
Die Deutsche Nationalbibliothek verzeichnet diese Publikation in der Deutschen Nationalbibliografie; detaillierte bibliografische Daten sind im Internet über http://dnb.dnb.de abrufbar

1. Auflage 2018

www.klett-lerntraining.de
Umschlagfoto: ullstein bild, Berlin
Abbildungen: S. 6: Zeichnung von Steffen Jähde, Sundhagen; S. 99: Laura Huxley, *This Timeless Moment. A Personal View of Aldous Huxley*, San Francisco: Mercury House, 1991, S. 240; S. 122: Shutterstock (Chantal de Bruijne), New York; S. 138: Felix Mussil/CCC, www.c5.net
Satz: DOPPELPUNKT, Stuttgart
Druck: medienhaus Plump GmbH, Rheinbreitbach
Printed in Germany
ISBN 978-3-12-923146-3

1 Introduction

2 Analysis and Interpretation

1 Introduction

Aún aprendo (I am still learning).
FRANCISCO DE GOYA
(Huxley's motto)

Aldous Huxley's *Brave New World* written in 1931 is one of the most fascinating and interesting dystopian novels. The future nightmare presented by the author still arouses the interest of a wide readership and challenges them to reflect on the ideas, themes and problems dealt with in the novel that also seem to be relevant today. Huxley's warning of the danger of a dehumanized future world includes such problems as the misuse of political power, sciences and technology, genetic engineering and cloning, world population growth, mass production and consumption, the manipulation of public opinion and the loss of cultural and ethical values. He insists on the human right of individual freedom and happiness against every kind of totalitarian oppression and open or hidden persuasion.
In order to understand *Brave New World*, it is helpful to know something about the author's life, time and works. In the following chapters of this study aid you are informed about the contents and the characters and offered an analysis and interpretation of the novel. Huxley's critical view of *Brave New World* and additional materials could support your critical approach to understanding the novel. Finally, the impulses and model tasks might inspire you to deal with its essential questions and problems.

The Author's Life, Time and Works

Aldous Huxley's life

Aldous Leonard Huxley was born in Godalming, a small town in Surrey, southwest of London, which among other places in Surrey (see map on p. 6) he mentions at the end of his dystopian novel *Brave New World* (p. 209) when he describes the protagonist's flight from London to his hermitage in Surrey. Huxley belonged to a famous and highly educated family. His grandfather was Thomas Henry Huxley (1825–1895), the great biologist and friend of Charles Darwin (1809–1892), who supported and publicized Darwin's ideas about evolution. As he enthusiastically and successfully defended Darwin's theory against creationist attacks, he ironically called himself "Darwin's bulldog". Aldous Huxley admired his grandfather and followed his fundamental scientific credo: "Sit down before fact like a little child, and be prepared to give up every preconceived notion, follow humbly wherever and

Southeast England

to whatever abysses Nature leads or you shall learn nothing. I have only begun to learn content and peace of mind since I have resolved at all risks to do this." (Laura Huxley, 1991, p. 330)
According to this statement, Aldous Huxley was interested in various fields of knowledge including arts and science, philosophy, culture and geography. He was born into the family of the famous literary critic Matthew Arnold (1822–1888), the highly esteemed writer, his aunt Humphrey Ward, born Arnold (1851–1920) and teachers such as Thomas Arnold (1795–1842), headmaster of Rugby Public School and both his parents, who endeavoured to enable their four children to get the best education possible, which meant to attend the elitist Eton College and the university in Oxford or Cambridge. Huxley's father Leonard was a public school teacher and became a publishing editor after having written a biography about his famous father T. H. Huxley. His wife founded her own school based on her idealistic and liberal educational principles, which Aldous attended at the age of seven. In 1903 he went to the boarding Prep School Hillside and in 1908 to Eton College.
In 1908 Aldous was deeply depressed by his mother's death from cancer shortly after he went to Eton following his elder brother Julian. At Eton College he had to translate English poetry into Latin and Greek and to write religious and philosophical essays. In his spare time he read the famous modern authors of his time such as Oscar Wilde and George Bernhard Shaw. As he was very much interested in science, especially in biology like his grandfather and his elder brother Julian, he wanted to study medicine and science but unfortunately could not realize his dream because of an eye disease that nearly caused his total blindness in 1911 and could only be prevented after several operations. Instead of studying medicine at Balliol College in Oxford, where his brother Trevenen studied mathematics, he enrolled there to study English literature and philosophy after his study trips to Marburg in 1911 and to Grenoble in 1913. Because of his thirst for knowledge and his friendly character he was soon the centre of a group of students with the same kind of interests. They discussed serious and frivolous themes and were particularly fascinated by Jazz, which Aldous also played on the piano.
Whereas his brother Julian (1887–1975) went to America and became a professor of zoology, then director of London Zoo and General director of UNESCO, his over-ambitious and extremely scrupulous brother Trevenen committed suicide in 1914 when he could not marry the girl he loved because of the strict social conventions of his time. Aldous could never get over the three strokes of fate: the early death of his mother followed by the breaking-up of his family, his near-blindness and his brother's suicide, which among other motifs taken from his life are alluded to in his dystopian novel *Brave New World*, for instance eye-sickness ("ophthalmia", p. 100), Linda's death (Chapter Fourteen) and John's suicide at the end of the novel.

As Aldous was declared unfit for military service because of his bad eyesight at the beginning of World War I, he continued his literary studies at Balliol College, passed the final examinations with distinction in 1916 and – after a short time as a stand-in teacher at the public school in Repton – he began his eight months' alternative service at the estate of Lady Ottoline and Philip Morrell in Garsington near Oxford. Philipp Morrell was one of the few Members of Parliament who voted against sending British troops to France in World War I and accommodated conscientious objectors. As Garsington was also a meeting place of renowned philosophers, writers, men of letters and economists such as Bertrand Russell, D. H. Lawrence, Katherine Mansfield, Virginia Woolf, T. S. Eliot, Middleton Murray and Mainard Keynes, Aldous Huxley had the opportunity to meet them and discuss various topics and thus broaden his encyclopaedic knowledge.

In 1926 he and D. H. Lawrence, who also informed him about the Indians' life in New Mexico, an important topic of *Brave New World*, became friends. A year after his friend's death Huxley began to write the dystopian novel, which he finished in four months though as usual he considerably revised the first draft. Bertrand Russell, the best known British philosopher of the 19th century, who as a pacifist lost his job as a lecturer at Cambridge University because of his public call for objection against the war, aroused Huxley's interest in pacifism. Russell was awarded the Nobel Prize for Literature in 1950 and is the author of the book *The Scientific Outlook*, one of the most important sources for Huxley's dystopia.

At Garsington Huxley also made acquaintance with the 17-year-old Maria Nys, a refugee from Belgia, who had found shelter in Lady Ottoline's home in 1915 and whom he married four years later after having given up several jobs such as the job as a teacher at Eton because of his bad eyesight and the lack of pedagogical skills. In 1916 he began to publish some volumes of poetry and in 1919 he became a literary critic writing numerous reviews about books and theatre productions for Middleton Murray's literary weekly *The Athenaeum*. He also wrote critical articles and essays about many different topics such as architecture, ecology, social questions, fashion, gardening, etc for various magazines, which proved his ability to deal with other but literary and scientific themes and helped to develop his lucid essayistic style. Several of these themes and activities are also reflected in *Brave New World*. When for instance Helmholtz Watson, one of the main characters, is dissatisfied with his writing propaganda texts and wishes to be able to write something meaningful and relevant, Huxley alludes to his former writing advertising slogans.

After 1921 – his son Matthew was born a year before – Aldous and his family lived in Florence and Forte dei Marmi, Italy, since living costs were cheaper there and his father, who had to provide for his second wife and several children, was no longer able to support Aldous financially. He decided to become a freelance writer. In 1923 he made a contract with the publishing house Chatto & Windus, London and was supposed to write two books a year. As travelling and coming into contact with different cultures was one of his greatest pleasures, he went to Italy and France and started for a world trip to India, Indonesia, the Philippines, Hongkong, Japan and the USA. In 1925 he moved to Suresne and Sanary-sur-Mer in France, travelled by car through Spain and central America, returned to London for two years, stayed with D. H. Lawrence in New Mexico and finally settled down in California in 1937, where he lived at different places such as a ranch near the Mojave desert, Hollywood and Los Angeles. In Hollywood he was soon surrounded by inspiring friends such as Charlie Chaplin, Greta Garbo, Gary Cooper, Walt Disney, the famous astronomer Edwin Hubble and the Indian philosopher Krishnamurti. Though Huxley wrote some film scripts, for instance about Madame Curie, a film and theatre version of his short story *The Gioconda Smile* and the film adaptation of Jane Austen's novel *Pride and Prejudice*, he was not really successful.

In 1939 Huxley became interested in Eastern religions, mysticism and philosophies such as Hinduism and Buddhism and was fascinated by the ideas of contemplation, equanimity, non-violence, compassion and helpfulness.

After 1948 he continued travelling, for instance to Europe, Egypt, Jerusalem, Beirut, Cyprus and Peru. In 1953, in the McCarthy era, he applied for the American citizenship but was not accepted because he was only willing to declare that he refused to serve in the American army because of philosophical and not religious reasons. In 1961 his house together with his library of 6000 books and all his documents was destroyed by a bushfire. In the same year he went on a tour through Europe and to New Delhi to take part in the anniversary celebrations for the Indian poet and philosopher Rabindranath Tagore (1861–1941), who propagated the idea of reconciliation and had been awarded the Nobel Prize for Literature in 1913.

As Huxley had become a well-known writer of novels and essays, he was frequently invited to give lectures in the USA, Italy, Brazil, and several European cities. He took part in several international congresses such as the Congress of the World Academy of Arts and Sciences in Brussels (1962) and Stockholm (1963). In 1960 he became a visiting professor at the Menninger Foundation in Topeka and the Massachusetts Institute of Technology (MIT) in Boston and in 1962 a research professor at the University of California at Berkeley. In 1959 he won the Award of Merit for the Novel by the American Academy of Arts and Letters and in 1962 the title "Companion of Literature" of the Royal Society of Literature, one of the highest literary awards in Britain. A year after his beloved first wife's death from breast cancer in 1955 he married the Italian psychotherapist and writer Laura Archera, who supported his various activities and also took part in his psychodelic sessions and drug experiments. But when in 1963 Huxley was asked to accept the presidency of

a foundation for research in LSD, he refused: "The last thing I want is to create an image of myself as 'Mr. LSD'; nor have I the least desire (being without any talent for this kind of thing) to get involved in the politics of psychedelics. [...] I am not a medical man, nor a psychotherapist, nor a research worker, nor an evangelist; and I am neither an organizer, nor a sitter on committees, nor a forensic orator. I am a man of letters who can work only in solitude, a writer on a great diversity of themes, of which LSD is only one. This being so, it would be very foolish of me to accept the presidency of your group." (Quoted from: Laura Huxley, 1991, pp. 137 f)
In March 1963 he took part in the Congress of the UN-Food and Agriculture Organization in Rome and had a private audience with Pope Johannes XXIII. He died on November 22nd from tongue cancer, which had been treated in vain since 1960. Two days before he died he expressed his insatiable thirst for knowledge and the extension of his consciousness by whispering: "It is never enough. Never enough." (Laura Huxley, 1991, p. 67)

Aldous Huxley's works and their historical background

Aldous Huxley was born into a highly intellectual family who was eager to learn about the new scientific theories and the development of arts. The Victorian Age, which ended with Queen Victoria's death in 1901, was characterized by the growing power of Britain and her Empire, the progress of science and technology with their positive and negative social consequences, and the predominant values of sexual morality, family loyalty, thrift, sobriety and hard work. The living standard of the upper and middle classes was rising continuously, the working classes, however, still lived in poverty and did not have many chances to get a better education and improve their situation. "[...] the social problem was not at its end but at its beginning, and might well in the coming century devour the other aspects of political life" (Trevelyan, 1988, p. 522).
Until the Second World War the British society was still divided into three different classes, the upper class (the aristocracy and wealthy people), the middle class subdivided into upper middle class, middle class and lower middle class, and the working class. They were separated from each other because of their different living standards, education, work and even their different forms of the English language. In *Brave New World* Huxley criticizes the traditional British class distinction by dividing the dystopian society into five castes of people who – according to their different intellectual and physical conditioning – are content with their qualified or unqualified work and their demanding or primitive living conditions. As Aldous Huxley belonged to a rather wealthy and educated family, his parents sent him to a boarding school and then to the elitist Eton College, which he also satirizes in his dystopia as a privileged school for Alpha and Beta students.

Huxley describes and analyzes the political, social and scientific developments and phenomena of his time in a critically and also satirical way. In his early wittily satirical novels *Crome Yellow* (1921), *Antic Hay* (1923) and *Point Counter Point* (1928) Huxley describes and analyzes the intellectual decadence and moral corruption of his contemporary society, the desire for fun and amusement during the so-called roaring twenties of the 20th century. *Brave New World*, which he wrote in only four months in 1931, was published in 1932 and soon became a bestseller. Until today it has remained a "longseller" since many of Huxley's futuristic ideas, which appeared to him already implicit in his time, are considered also relevant nowadays such as his warning of the loss of individual freedom through state control, genetic engineering and cloning, the dependence on technology and alienation from nature, entertainment and diversion, mass consumption, the manipulation of the personal and public opinion e.g. through the mass media, etc.
Huxley's dystopia is often compared with George Orwell's dystopian novel *1984*, which was written after World War II in 1948. After Stalin's and Hitler's tyranny and the deaths of more than 55 millions of people during the Second World War, the extinction of more than 6 million Jewish people in German concentration camps, the purges under Stalin that killed millions of Russians and the many other war crimes, Orwell portrays a future world of brutal dictatorship, terror and perpetual warfare. Huxley's dystopia, however, was written before Stalin's and Hitler's tyranny. He describes a future world of biochemically conditioned people who are programmed from birth to death to enjoy work, consumption, promiscuity, shallow entertainment, and live in permanent peace and comfort. Huxley stresses his concern about the dangers of moral decline and human manipulation in a scientific and technological civilization. His main interest was to make people aware of the danger of the loss of individual freedom, which he deals with in numerous essays and in *Brave New World Revisited* (1958). In this collection of essays he criticizes some aspects of his dystopian novel and treats topics such as overpopulation, over-organization, propaganda, subconscious persuasion and mind-manipulation techniques and also compares Orwell's novel with his *Brave New World*:

> "In 1931 systematic terrorism was not the obsessive contemporary fact which it had become in 1984, and the future dictatorship of my imaginary world was a good deal less brutal than the future dictatorship so brilliantly portrayed by Orwell. In the context of 1948, *1984* seemed dreadfully convincing. But tyrants, after all, are mortal and circumstances change. Recent developments in Russia, and recent advances in science and technology, have robbed Orwell's book of some of its gruesome verisimilitude. A nuclear war will, of course, make nonsense of everybody's predictions. But assuming for the moment that the Great Powers can somehow refrain from destroying us, we can say that it now looks as though the odds were more in favour of something like *Brave New World* than of something like *1984*." (Huxley, *Brave New World Revisited*, 1994, pp. 4 f)

In his dystopian novel *Ape and Essence* (1948), which is an extremely satirical successor to *Brave New World*, Huxley presents the future world of a perverted American society after an atomic war without love, worshipping the Devil, burning all the books, since "between World War II and World War III people amused themselves with power politics" with the consequence of "[w]orse malnutrition for more people. More political unrest, resulting in more aggressive nationalism and imperialism. [...] And why did they choose to destroy themselves? Because that was what Belial wanted them to do [...]." (Huxley, *Ape and Essence*, 2008, p. 131)
In 1946 he published *Science, Liberty and Peace*, a collection of essays, in which he beseeches the scientists who became guilty of mass destruction during the war not to give in to the goals of politicians and businessmen but reflect critically on their research. He continued writing numerous essays about various themes, e.g. about art in the Baroque period, about artists such as El Greco and Goya and about philosophers, which he published in his book *Themes and Variations* in 1950. As his bad eyesight improved after the Bates method of exercises, he propagated it in his essay *The Art of Seeing* (1942). In 1952 he published *The Devils of Loudun*, a study of the customs and morals of France in the 17th century, which was also adapted for the screen and inspired the dramatist John Whiting to write the play *The Devils* and the famous Polish composer Krzysztof Penderecki to compose an opera.
As Huxley tried to get to the bottom of things and extend his consciousness and perception, he became interested in mysticism and parapsychology in the last years of his life. He also began to experiment with drugs from 1953 on, which critics believe to have been rather extravagant and dangerous leading to a dead end. In his letter to Ida Herz (March 21st, 1954) Thomas Mann severely condemned Huxley's book *The Doors of Perception* (1954) about his friend's drug experiments, which had been published only a month before he read it. He believed that it was irresponsible and contributed to the stultification of the world and to man's inability of treating the serious problems of his time sensibly.
Huxley's interest in oriental and European mysticism is expressed in such novels as *Eyeless in Gaza* (1936), *After Many a Summer Dies the Swan* (1939), *Grey Eminence* (1941) and *Time Must Have a Stop* (1944), in his introduction to a translation of *Bhagavad-Gita*, one of the most important Hindu sacred books, and in his *Perennial Philosophy* (1945), where he comes to the conclusion that all Eastern and Western religious and philosophical wisdom has the same goal, the reconciliation of religion and science.
He describes his experiments with mescaline and other hallucinogenic drugs to heighten perception in *The Doors of Perception* (1954) and *Heaven and Hell* (1956). He tried to find a drug or a dose without physically negative side-effects, which he had already described in *Brave New World*, where the dystopian society is controlled by regular and different doses of soma, a

fictitious "harmless" drug, which produces artificial happiness and makes people content with their lack of freedom. But Huxley also describes the misuse of soma by the protagonist's mother Linda, who dies from a frequent over-dose at the early age of 44, and warns of the dangers of uncontrolled experiments with drugs in an appendix to *The Devils of Loudun* (1952).
Whereas in *Brave New World* the drug called soma was used to make people artificially happy, Huxley approved of a perfected LSD drug used for religious purposes in his last novel *Island* (1962), which he considered a good Utopia, a vision of an Eastern state of reason and love. Before he felt competent enough to write this Utopian novel in five years, he needed 20 years of research including Greek history, Polynesian anthropology, translations from Sanskrit and Buddhist sources, scientific books about pharmacology, neurophysiology, psychology, education and numerous literary works and travel books, which underscores his thirst for knowledge and the relevance of his lifelong motto: *Aún aprendo* – "I am still learning" (cf. Laura Huxley, 1991, p. 287).

2 Analysis and Interpretation

Brave New World: Contents and Commentary

Huxley's dystopia *Brave New World* written in 1931 in only four months and published in 1932 has become his most successful novel. It is set in A.F. 632, i.e. 632 years after Henry Ford's birth in 1863 or AD 2495 and presents a future world based on Ford's principle of mass production and mass consumption. Whereas Ford successfully introduced the assembly line and specialized work to produce the Model T car (1908–1927), in the brave new world all inhabitants are industrially produced, biochemically manipulated and psychologically conditioned to be content with their different roles in society and their specialized work.
A number of topics Huxley deals with in his novel are still being discussed nowadays, for instance the misuse of political power, science and technology, genetic engineering, cloning, world populaton growth and food supply, mass consumption and the influence of mass media on opinion-forming, the endangering of arts, religion and ethics in society, etc. The description of a future world state, in which people are conditioned and manipulated from birth to death, is meant to be a warning of those forces and developments that could lead to the loss of individual freedom.
In the first three chapters of the novel Huxley describes the principles on which the dystopian society is based. The reader is introduced into this brave new world by two powerful characters, the Director of the Conditioning Centre and the Controller of the Western World.

Chapter One
The novel begins like a movie showing a high-rise building, the Central London Hatchery and Conditioning Centre. On a shield you can read the motto of the world state: Community, Identity, Stabilitity. In a large cold laboratory on the ground floor workers in white overalls are silently controlling tubes.
The Director of Hatcheries and Conditioning begins to explain what is going on in the huge laboratory to a group of male students who automatically put down everything the Director tells them word by word. "The boys scribbled like mad." (p. 8) They learn that the inhabitants of the brave new world are no longer naturally born but industrially produced. The ovaries from females are surgically removed, kept alive in incubators, inspected for abnormalities and then artificially fertilized in glass containers filled with sperms. Whereas the fertilized ova of the Alphas and Betas, the most intelligent beings of the brave new world, remain in the incubator until they are bottled, the Gammas,

Deltas and Epsilons, the less intelligent and even unintelligent beings, undergo the so-called Bokanovsky Process. Contrary to the Alphas and Betas, who are produced from a single egg and thus develop to an individual embryo and adult, the fertilized eggs of the Gammas, Deltas and Epsilons are made proliferate up to ninety-six identical embryos that develop to ninety-six identical beings. Because of the so-called Podsnap's Technique it is even possible to accelerate the process of the ripening of mature eggs and produce thousands of identical twins, sometimes even 15 000 twins from one ovary. As in other Hatchery Centres of the World State even more identical twins are produced, the Director wants to break their record.
He tells the students that the mass production of identical beings is meant to guarantee a stable community, according to the world state's motto. The cloned embryos grow inside bottles, are tested for sex and accordingly labelled as male, female or freemartin, since only about thirty percent of the female embryos are allowed to develop normally in order to guarantee fresh ovaries whereas the rest is treated with male sex-hormone to become sterile.
All the bottles move on production lines from the Bottling Room to the Social Predestination Room where they are predestined and conditioned for specific functions in society. Contrary to the Alphas and Betas, who receive the most oxygen to become intelligent, Epsilons only get little oxygen to condition them for unqualified work. Other embryos are heat-conditioned for tropical work, conditioned to tolerate unhealthy chemicals in order to become chemical workers or by constant rotation become astronauts. Finally, after 267 days the babies are released from their bottles, i.e. "decanted" in the Decanting Room. The Director tells the students that conditioning aims at making people like the work they are destined to do throughout their lives. It is "the secret of happiness and virtue" (p. 19). He also informs the students about experiments to produce beings who are fully grown and sexually mature at an earlier age. But such experiments have not yet been satisfyingly successful. As the Director is in a hurry, the students are not shown the production of the Alpha and Beta embryos but are asked to follow him to the Nurseries where the children are psychologically conditioned.

Chapter Two

On a notice board the students read: Infant Nurseries. Neo-Pavlovian Conditioning Rooms, which alludes to the Russian scientist Ivan Pavlov (1849–1936) and his work on animal conditioning. They enter a large and bright room where Nurses are placing numerous rose bowls on the floor and – according to the Director's order – a lot of colourful children's books. Then the nurses bring in eight-month-old babies dressed in khaki, all of them identical Deltas, who joyfully crawl to the roses and books but are frequently

terrorized by shrill alarm bells, sirens, explosions and electric shocks as soon as they touch the flowers and books, until they are terribly frightened of them and conditioned to hate them as long as they live. Thus they are prevented from reading the "wrong books" in the future since that might endanger the stability of the brave new world. The babies are conditioned to dislike flowers because instead of loving nature, lower-caste people have to love the use of elaborate apparatus in country sports and public transport, e.g. trains to increase mass consumption and mass production. The Director cynically comments on this misuse of Pavlov's theories saying: "What man has joined, nature is powerless to put asunder." (p. 23)
The Director tells the students that in former times, when "Our Ford" (instead of "Our Lord", i.e. Jesus), who invented the automobile assembly line, was still alive and dead languages such as French, German and Polish were still spoken, human beings had parents and were naturally born. The students are shocked by the words 'parent', 'mother', 'father' and 'born', which have become obscene in the brave new world. The Director confirms their reaction as correct and stresses that not only family life but "most historical facts *are* unpleasant" (p. 19).
He informs them about the discovery of sleep-teaching or hypnopaedia in Poland 23 years after Ford had started the mass production of his T-Model cars. While the Polish boy Reuben was sleeping, a lecture given by George Bernard Shaw was broadcast by a London radio station and when the child woke up he was able to repeat the lecture word by word in English, a language he had not learned before. But as it was wrongly assumed that sleep-teaching could be used for intellectual education and was therefore abandoned, in the brave new world it has been successfully applied in moral education since A.F. 214 (AD 2077). Thus the reader already learns that in the brave new world the Christian creed and the Christian calendar were replaced by the belief in Ford and accordingly by a new calendar.
The students are led into a dormitory where eighty sleeping Alpha children are taught Elementary Class Consciousness. A whispering voice permanently repeats that Gamma, Delta and Epsilon children are stupid, that Alphas are more intelligent than Betas and that the different castes can be distinguished by the different colours of their clothes, since Alphas are dressed in grey, Betas in red, Gammas in green, Deltas in khaki and Epsilons in black. The Director praises hypnopaedia as the "greatest moralizing and socializing force of all time" (p. 29), which the students immediately write down in their note books. When the Director finally shouts that the child's and therefore also the adult's mind are only made up of the World State's suggestions, he triumphantly bangs the table and thus involuntarily wakes the children.

Chapter Three

After being shown the biological, chemical and psychological conditioning of brave new world's children, the students watch how the children learn to consume elaborate games that require much apparatus and sexual games with different children to become already promiscuous at an early age. One of the boys who is not willing to join the sexual game is taken to a psychologist to find out whether he is abnormal. The students give an incredulous laugh when the Director tells them that a long time before and after Ford children and even young people not yet twenty were not allowed to amuse themselves sexually. Suddenly the Controller Mustapha Mond appears and is welcomed by the Director.

The following part of this chapter is a sort of montage of different scenes and statements of some of the main characters of the novel in an unusual combination, which are summarized here according to the main characters, whose roles in the brave new world and their attitudes towards it are displayed.

In the first scene Henry Foster and his Assistant Predestinator show their dislike of Bernard Marx when they meet in the lift after work while the production of future men and women continues and is controlled by the following shift. Henry asks his assistant whether he also intends to go to the "Feelies" (movies with tactual effects) to watch sexual scenes. Whereas Henry is looking forward to watching the film, Bernard Marx shows contempt because he dislikes such superficial films. He is also shocked to hear that Henry Foster encourages the Assistant Predestinator to have sex with Lenina, whom he praises as "wonderfully pneumatic" (p. 44) and whom he considers "a bit of meat" only (p. 45), which Lenina herself thinks to be as Bernard Marx believes (cf. p. 45). When Henry Foster realizes Bernard's sullenness, he offers him a gramme of soma, the drug that is commonly used in the brave new world whenever somebody feels sad or depressed. But Bernard refuses to take it and would like to kill them whom he finally calls "Idiots, swine!" (p. 53). Henry Foster hurries to his helicopter to play Obstacle Golf with Lenina.

After work Lenina Crowne goes by lift to the girls' dressing room, where she also meets her friend Fanny, whose second name is the same because there are only about ten thousand different names for the world's population, which is kept stabile at about two billion people. The room is crowded and filled with a hundred baths and massage machines. The girls have to talk at the pitch of their voices to drown the synthetic music. After the bath Lenina chooses one of the perfumes coming out of tubes and uses one of the massage machines. When Fanny tells her that she is going to have a "pregnancy substitute" to feel well the next three or four years, Lenina is astonished that the doctor allowed it since she is not yet twenty-one. Fanny, however, disapproves Lenina's going out only with Henry Foster instead of changing artners and warns her that the Director would be furious if he knew se not being promiscuous is against the rules of the brave new world. As Henry Foster changes his partners frequently, Fanny calls him a "perfect gentleman", who is always correct and strictly "conventional" (p. 42). Everyone should try to be promiscuous even if he or she does not feel like it since "everybody belongs to everyone else" (p. 43). But she is horrified when Lenina tells her that Bernard Marx has asked her to accompany him to the Savage Reservation, and that she finds him "sweet" though he cuts himself off from them most of the time. Fanny believes that he is ugly, because for an Alpha Plus he is too small and looks like a Gamma. It is said that somebody had put alcohol into the blood-surrogate by mistake when he grew up in the bottle. Nevertheless, Lenina intends to accept his invitation to go to the Reservation. Finally, she puts on her fashionable clothes and a contraceptive Malthusian belt. Fanny also wants to buy a new one instead of her old belt, according to the hypnopaedic slogans "I love new clothes" and "Ending is better than mending" (p. 50), which subconsciously influence the inhabitants of the brave new world to consume much in order to promote industrial production.

Whereas the behaviour and talks of Henry Foster, Bernard Marx, Lenina and Fanny Crowne serve as a link to the action in the following chapters, a large part of Chapter Three refers to the Resident Controller for Western Europe, Mustapha Mond, who explains fundamental principles of the World State to the students – and readers. Against that background, the reader can better understand the reasons of the main characters' talk and behaviour. That is why Huxley just lists different statements without mentioning the persons who utter them. Moreover, he repeats some hypnopaedic slogans such as "Ending is better than mending" several times to underline the conditioning and manipulation of the characters' words and behaviour with the exception of Bernard Marx, who seems to have remained an individual to a certain extent since his feelings deviate from the predestined views and behaviour of Henry Foster. To a certain extent, this also applies to Lenina Crowne, contrary to her friend Fanny.

The students can hardly believe that his fordship Mustapha Mond, one of the Ten World Controllers, stays with them to explain the system and the fundamental principles of the brave new world. He begins with stressing Ford's statement that "History is bunk" and lists ancient cultures, religions, names, buildings, compositions, etc, which are now forgotten such as ancient Greece and Rome, Odysseus, Jesus, Shakespeare's Lear, the French philosopher Pascal, cathedrals, symphonies, etc. As historical knowledge is considered useless, history is no longer taught to the students. But the Director knows that Mond himself still keeps old books such as the Bible and poetry in a safe in his study though it is strictly forbidden to read them in the brave new world. Mond asks the students to imagine what it was like to have a mother and live

with a family in one's home. But the boys are not able to do so because family life has been abolished in the brave new world. When Mond compares home to a dark, unhealthy and stinking prison overcrowded with a large family, one of the students nearly gets sick, and when Mond describes the emotional relationships between the members of the family in a repulsive way, the boys shudder. Referring to "Our Freud" Mond tells them that family life was the reason why there was "every kind of perversion from sadism to chastity", "madness and suicide" (p. 39). He also devaluates marriage and individual love because in the brave new world "everybody belongs to everyone else", which the students confirm since they all were hypnopaedically conditioned to take this slogan as self-evident (cf. p. 34).
According to Mond, the "poor pre-moderns" were not able to take things easily, they suffered pain and poverty, had strong emotions, were individually isolated and therefore not "sane, virtuous and happy" (p. 41). Thus Mond changes the proper meaning of the words in order to defend the conditioned and "stable" life in the brave new world. He underlines that there is "no social stability without individual stability" (p. 42). Industry does not need people with strong individual emotions of love, pain, religious feelings, complaints about old age and poverty but only "sane men, obedient men, stable in contentment" (ibid.). Stability is the central idea of the brave new world and the main principle of the life and death of its inhabitants. That is why they are conditioned – as far as possible – to be free from emotions (cf. p. 42).
Mond continues criticizing the ancestors who believed in a Christian God, individual liberty, democracy, and who levied war against each other and suffered economic collapse (Huxley's allusion to the great financial crash in 1929 and the following economic depression). Mond tells the students that in the Nine Years' War, which began in A.F. 141 (AD 2004), not only TNT but also biological bombs and gas weapons (an allusion to the First World War) were used and millions of people killed and historical buildings "luckily" destroyed (cf. p. 50). After the Nine Years' War, it was necessary to decide between total destruction and world control. At first the World Controllers tried to establish a stable world order by shooting opponents and destroying museums and gassing "two thousand culture fans" during the "famous British Museum Massacre" (p. 49) until they realized that instead of using force it was better to practise the "methods of ectogenesis [in-vitro fertilization], neo-Pavlovian conditioning and hypnopaedia" (ibid.). As the decision was for enduring stability, i.e. peace, production and consumption, the brave new world was founded based on total biological and mental control from birth to death. The Christian God was replaced by Our Ford and the cross by the T after cutting off its top. Instead of Christian services there are Ford's Day Celebrations, Community Sings and Solidarity Services. Instead of believing in Heaven and the immortality of the soul, two thousand pharmacologists and biochemists started in A.F. 178 to develop the perfect drug soma, a

euphoric, narcotic, pleasantly hallucinatory drug without dangerous side-effects. It has been produced commercially since A.F. 184 and everybody in the brave new world gets it for free whenever he or she wishes to feel well. Even old age has been overcome since people in the brave new world don't change when they get old; they continue to enjoy sex, work, consumption and distraction.
At the end of Chapter III, the Director angrily chases away some children who are playing sex games, which the Controller comments on: "Poor little children!"

Chapter Four

Part 1
Now Huxley continues the story of Lenina Crowne and Bernard Marx. Both seem to be the protagonists of the novel since Bernard falls in love with Lenina, who as a pretty and popular girl had sex with a lot of Alphas though she does not find some of them really attractive. When she meets Bernard in the lift from the changing rooms crowded with Alphas, she wants to talk to him about their visit to the Savage Reservation in New Mexico. She directly asks him in public if he wants to have her and cannot understand why Bernard flushes. Though Bernard is too small for an Alpha and therefore considered "ugly", Lenina likes him.
When they reach the roof of the high-rise building and the Epsilon-Minus liftman opens the gates, he awakes from his indifference and enjoys the sunlight but is apathetic again as soon as the lift goes down. As Lenina has a date with Henry Foster and wants to play Obstacle Golf with him, she runs to the helicopter hangar on top of the skyscraper while Bernard and Benito Hoover, who is permanently good-humoured without taking soma, admire Lenina's beauty.
When Lenina is flying with Henry Foster in his helicopter to the Obstacle Golf field, she sees a Red Rocket arriving from New York and looks down on London's skyscrapers, the satellite suburbs, several sports grounds where different castes are playing high-tech games, the Feely Studio, Delta and Epsilon road workers and the small town of the Television Corporation factory, where the different castes from Beta Minuses to Epsilons must use different caste-specific means of transportation after the shift. The higher castes use helicopters and the lower castes monorail tramcars. Lenina, who is a Beta Minus, is glad that she is not a Gamma.

Part 2
Bernard Marx feels miserable because he is not able to behave like the other inhabitants of the brave new world, who just follow the rules. He is annoyed when he realizes that the Epsilon hangar workers do not really respect him as an Alpha, since he is too small and looks like a Gamma. He feels an outsider

and isolated because he is mocked by lower-caste people. When he is sitting in his plane to visit his friend Helmholtz Watson, who works in the Propaganda House, Huxley describes the different offices in the sixty-storey building in Fleet Street, an allusion to the street in London where in Huxley's time several major newspapers had their offices. In the brave new world different papers are produced for the different castes such as a demanding paper for the upper caste and a paper for the lower castes that are only able to understand one-syllable words. TV, movies and synthetic music are produced in the Bureaux of Propaganda and the top floors are used by the College of Emotional Engineering.

Helmholtz Watson is described as a perfect Alpha Plus, who as an Emotional Engineer is a lecturer, journalist for the Alpha paper, and a writer of film scripts for the production of "feelies", slogans and hypnopaedic rhymes, all of them propaganda to manipulate people and to contribute to the brave new world's stability. But whereas Bernard Marx suffers from his physical defect, Helmholtz Watson is intellectually "defective" since he has been given too much oxygen when he was in the bottle and consequently is too intelligent for an Alpha. The two friends feel dissatisfied and isolated in the brave new world because, contrary to the other inhabitants, they are individuals (cf. p. 64). Helmholtz is extremely successful in every field of activity but is dissatisfied with his work, women, sports, etc. He feels that he has something important to say and the power to say it (cf. p. 66), but he doesn't yet know what it is.

After a short flight to Bernard's room, Helmholtz tries to express why he is dissatisfied with his propaganda texts and asks himself what there might be more important to say. He tries hard to make use of his power but his being conditioned as an Alpha seems to limit his creativity. He is unable to imagine themes that surpass the limits of propaganda and he therefore asks himself: "Can you say something about nothing?" (p. 66) Bernard believes there is somebody at the door overhearing their talk but he is mistaken. His statement "When people are suspicious with you, you start being suspicious with them" (p. 66) underlines that as an outsider in the brave new world he feels nervous and endangered. When he pities himself, Helmholtz feels sorry for "poor little Bernard" and wishes that he "would show a little more pride" (p. 66).

Thus Huxley points out that the goal of total stability has not been achieved in the brave new world since some of the characters such as Bernard and Helmholtz feel dissatisfied with their social roles due to mistakes in the process of their production. They are able to feel and express emotions, e.g. love, pity and compassion, and believe they are individuals and therefore outsiders. Huxley foreshadows their banishment from the brave new world by Mustapha Mond at the end of the novel by giving several hints in the first chapters.

Chapter Five

Part 1

While the lower-caste golfers are returning to London in monorail trains, Lenina and Henry start home in their helicopter and fly over a huge agricultural factory in Farnham, Surrey, and the crematorium in Slough, where the inhabitants of the brave new world are burnt after death to produce an enormous amount of phosphorous used as fertilizer. Henry is proud of that achievement since "we can go on being socially useful even after we're dead" (p. 68). When Lenina finds it strange that Alphas and Betas do not contain more phosphorous than the lower castes, Henry replies: "All men are physico-chemically equal", a perverted version of the fundamental human right expressed in the American Declaration of Independence: "[…] all men are created equal". When Henry underlines that "even Epsilons perform indispensible services" (p. 68), Lenina remembers the endless hypnopaedic repetitions of "Everyone works for everyone else. We can't do without anyone. Even Epsilons are useful. We couldn't do without Epsilons" (p. 68). Henry explains that the different castes are all conditioned to be content with their particular roles in society, which also applies to Lenina who is glad that she is not an Epsilon.
When the crematorium's output of hot gas makes the helicopter suddenly rise and afterwards fall, Lenina is delighted, whereas Henry is sad and wishes to know who it was that went up in hot gas, which alludes to the fact that even Henry Foster is able to feel compassion. He comforts himself by the hypnopaedic slogan "Everybody's happy now" (p. 69), which Lenina repeats. After landing on the roof of Henry's apartment skyscraper, they have an excellent meal and soma in the large dining-hall, go dancing in the Westminster Abbey Cabaret and enjoy the colour organ, the music of the "Sixteen Sexophonists" (mind the wordplay!), and the favourite piece of music with the lines: "There ain't no Bottle in all the world like that dear little Bottle of mine" or "Bottle of mine, it's you I've always wanted!" (pp. 71 f) After the last dance, a "Malthusian Blues" played by the "Synthetic Music apparatus", a loudspeaker politely asks the dancers to leave. Lenina and Henry take the lift up to Henry's room to spend the night together. Huxley sharply contrasts the artificial and synthetic dancing hall with nature. But neither before nor after the dance Lenina and Henry are able see the beautiful starlight because either the stars cannot be seen because of the bright electric signs and advertising or they ignore the stars since they are high on soma.

Part 2

Bernard Marx flies to the "Fordson Community Singery", a skyscraper on the site of the former St Paul's Cathedral, to take part in his fortnightly "Solidarity Service", which in the brave new world replaces the former Christian service. As he is a bit late, he takes a seat beside a girl he dislikes and regrets that he

does not sit beside one of the beautiful girls. Six men and six women alternately form a circle and are expected to lose their identities and fuse into a greater being. The repetition of the President's sign of the T, the permanent synthetic music, the singing of long Solidarity Hymns ("For I am you and you are I", p. 76) and the drinking of soma turn them into a state of ecstasy until they feel the appearance of Ford. They start dancing and stamping to the rhythm of the loud synthetic music which becomes faster and faster until they sing an orgiastic song and fall into a sexual orgy.
Bernard Marx, however, who is not able to give up his identity and only pretends to be fused into the greater being, feels disappointed and lonely. As an individual he cannot achieve the goal of the Solidarity Service, namely to become an integral part of the brave new world's community according to the world state's motto: Community, Identity, Stability (cf. p. 7).

Chapter Six

Part 1

Lenina finds Bernard "odd", because he does not always behave like a "normal", i.e. perfectly conditioned citizen of the brave new world. Though Lenina first hesitated to fly with Bernard to the Reservation and considered to go to the North Pole with funny Benito Hoover, she finally prefers to accompany Bernard to America since she already knows the North Pole and dislikes the primitive hotel there. Moreover, it is a rare chance to see the Reservation since as an Alpha Plus Bernard is one of the few people who is allowed to go there.
Bernard dislikes being in a crowd and wishes to go for a walk in the Lake District with Lenina and just talk to her. But Lenina is unable to understand Bernard since it is against her conditioning. She cannot imagine what they should talk about at such a lonely place.
When she persuades Bernard to fly to Amsterdam to watch the Women's Wrestling Championship, he feels miserable and rejects the glass of soma which Lenina offers him to cheer up. Instead, he gets angry about her hypnopaedic phrases and says: "I'd rather be myself" and "not somebody else, however jolly" (p. 82). On their way back to London Bernard stops the engine of the helicopter and wants to enjoy the windy weather at night and look at the moon and the sea because it makes him feel an individual and "not so completely part of something else" or like "a cell in the social body" (p. 83). But Lenina is horrified by such romantic words and switches on the radio. She is shocked by his "blasphemy" of wishing to be free and not enslaved by his conditioning (cf. p. 83) and is totally unable to understand his idea of individual freedom, since she feels free like everybody, according to the hypnopaedic slogan "Everybody's happy now" (p. 69). She suggests taking soma to be jolly again, which Bernard finally does before he goes to bed with her.

When they meet the next day, Bernard is depressed because Lenina really believes that she is "pneumatic" or just "meat". Like John, the Savage later on (cf. Chapters Nine and Twelve), Bernard would have liked to have sex with Lenina later and not already after their first meeting. Lenina, however, disqualifies such talk as "incomprehensible and dangerous" (p. 85) since it is against her conditioning. She also does not comprehend Bernard's wish to know what passion is. Whereas he wants "to feel something strongly", Lenina is only able to have "fun" (p. 85).

Part 2

When Bernard presents the permission to visit the Reservation in New Mexico signed by the World Controller to the Director, he is surprised because his superior tells him that he himself went to the Reservation at the age of Bernard about twenty years ago. Thus, also the Director violates a hypnopaedic prejudice never to talk about past times. Obviously, he still feels guilty since the girl who went with him got lost on the Reservation and he had to return without her. Now he is haunted by that loss in his dreams. When Bernard expresses sympathy, the Director realizes his mistake of telling about his relationship to the girl he obviously loved. So he defends himself by saying that their relationship was nothing emotional. He admits that he does not know why he told that "trivial anecdote" to Bernard, which proves that, contrary to his official behaviour, he is not always able to keep his emotions under control. They are still subconsciously present.
As the Director is angry about his mistake, he criticizes Bernard's deviating emotional behaviour and demands that he must conform to infantile emotions, even against his conditioning as an Alpha. In case he does not obey, the Director threatens to banish him to Iceland, which Bernard does not take seriously. Helmholtz Watson, however, dislikes Bernard's alternating inclination to boasting or self-pity.

Part 3

In the Blue Pacific Rocket Lenina and Bernard fly to New Orleans and over Texas to Santa Fé, where they spend the night in a luxury hotel with every modern technical comfort, which Lenina describes with the hypnopaedic slogan "progress is lovely" (p. 90). Though there is no scent tube, television and hot water on the Reservation, Lenina wants to go there. They meet the Warden of the Reservation, who describes it as a large region of five hundred and sixty thousand square kilometres, subdivided into four districts and surrounded by a high-tension wire fence which prevents any escape. The sixty thousand Indians and half-breeds were naturally born and live in families. As there is no contact to the civilized world, the people preserve their traditional habits and customs and believe in both Christianity and their own gods. They still speak languages such as Zuñi and Spanish that are

not known in the brave new world and suffer from diseases and have to be careful because of ferocious and venomous animals.
Lenina does not listen to the Warden's explanations since she has taken soma and Bernard is worried because he left the eau-de-Cologne tap open in his London bathroom. After the Warden's talk he rings up Helmholtz and asks him to turn it off. Helmholtz tells him that the Director has decided to send him to Iceland. This time it is a shock to Bernard and he takes soma.
A Reservation Guard flies Lenina and Bernard to a rest-house in Malpais and calms Lenina by saying that the savages are no longer dangerous since they were tamed by gas bombs.

Chapter Seven
When Bernard and Lenina are taken to the pueblo of Malpais, Lenina expresses her dislike of the guide and the place, since the Indian smells and the pueblo looks totally different from the high-rise buildings in London. Moreover, she hates walking and finds the Indians' half-nakedness, their headdress and being painted disgusting. She is shocked when she sees the dirt, rubbish, dust and flies at the entrance of the pueblo. Whereas Lenina cannot understand how people can live in such a way and repeats the hypnopaedic slogan "Cleanliness is next to fordliness", Bernard only shrugs his shoulders and ironically makes use of "the second hypnopaedic lesson in elementary hygiene": "Yes, and civilization is sterilization" (p. 98).
When they see an extremely old and toothless Indian, who is just skin and bones, Lenina is horrified and wishes that they had not visited the Reservation. Bernard hides his fright and explains that the inhabitants in the brave new world also grow old but look rather young until they die at the age of sixty. As their physical condition is permanently controlled, they are preserved from diseases and get transfusions of young blood. Lenina does not listen and as she forgot to take soma with her, she has to look at everything that is considered indecent in the brave new world, e.g. the breast-feeding of babies and the skin disease of an old woman. But Bernard, who pretends to be strong and unorthodox, says that people in the brave new world might regret that they are unable of having strong feelings, do not have a caring mother and – addressing Lenina – have never been a mother. Lenina only wants to leave the pueblo immediately.
When the Indian guide leads them away, they pass a dead dog on a rubbish heap, see a woman with a goitre killing lice in the hair of a little girl, walk through a terribly smelling room until they arrive at the village square crowded with Indians. As the rhythms of the drums remind Lenina of the synthetic sounds during the Solidarity Services, she likes them but as soon as the Indians' fierce and shrill songs are heard, which remind her of a lower-caste Community Sing, she is disgusted. When the Indians start the rain dance with snakes in their hands, the images of an eagle and a naked man

nailed to a cross appear and a young man is nearly whipped to death, Lenina is shocked to such an extent that Bernard cannot calm her at all. She only wishes to take soma.
Suddenly a young man welcomes them “in faultless but peculiar English” (p. 103). He is deeply disappointed that he was denied to be the sacrifice in the Indian ceremony because of his non-Indian complexion since he has a white skin and blond hair. When the Savage tells them that he would have been stronger than the other young man and could have suffered more blood loss, he uses a phrase taken from Shakespeare’s *Macbeth*: “The multitudinous seas incarnadine [get red with blood]”. This line is spoken by Macbeth after his murder of King Duncan (II,2,65), which proves the young man’s extraordinary knowledge of Shakespeare’s plays for the first time. (For further information concerning the quotations from Shakespeare’s works see p. 2 in this study aid.) Moreover, the Savage alludes to his being different from the pueblo Indians though he would like to be accepted by them and please their gods Pookong and Jesus (cf. pp. 103 f).
As Lenina smiles at the young man and makes him blush, they seem to like each other at first sight. When Bernard asks the Savage to tell his story, Lenina and Bernard learn that his mother Linda once came from the “Other Place” (the brave new world) with his father Tomakin, which Bernard at once recognizes as the Director’s pet name, since his first name is Thomas. As Linda had fallen down a steep place and hurt her head, his father could not find her and returned to the Other Place without her. She afterwards gave birth to her son, John the Savage.
When the Savage leads Lenina and Bernard to his home, a dirty and rather dilapidated house on the outskirts of the pueblo, Lenina is shocked by Linda, whom she finds even worse than the old man she met before. Linda’s outward appearance is disgusting, since she is extremely fat and ugly, looks unhealthy, wears dirty rags and smells of alcohol. As soon as she sees Bernard and Lenina, Linda embraces and kisses her. She is glad to see “civilized” faces and clothes again and tells about her shame when she had a baby and no soma but only mescal and peyotl, drugs that made her feel sick. She is not able to explain why she got pregnant because she had always applied contraceptive methods and there is no Abortion Centre on the Reservation. Though Linda, who is a Beta and has worked in the Fertilizing Room, is conditioned to live according hypnopaedic slogans such as “Civilization is Sterilization” and “The more stitches, the less riches” (p. 107), she has not been able to do so because there is no hot water and she had never learned to mend clothes in the brave new world. She believes that the Indians are lunatics and “everything they do is mad” (p. 107). Contrary to the hypnopaedic slogan “Everybody belongs to everyone else”, the Indians marry and therefore despised her since their husbands came to have sex with her until their wives cruelly beat her and

stopped her following the rules of the brave new world. Nevertheless, Linda admits that she likes her son though he had always been upset when a lover came and even tried to kill her lover Popé. She in vain tried to condition John according to the principles of the brave new world, but as a Beta, who only knew the work in the Fertilizing Room, she was not prepared to answer the boy's questions about how a helicopter works or who made the world.

Chapter Eight

Outside Linda's home Bernard tells her son John that he cannot understand the way of life on the Reservation with mothers, dirt, gods, old age, disease, etc, and asks the young Savage to tell the story of his life beginning as far back as he can remember. The first thing John remembers apart from the hot weather and the Indian food is that when he was a baby his mother sang lullabies she had learned in the brave new world such as "Bye, Baby Banting, soon you'll need decanting" (p. 109), which he liked but could not understand. As a boy he was frightened when Popé, a big Indian, visited his mother to have sex with her and carried him in another room before. John also remembers that his mother was thrown out of the Indian women's weaving room because she could not weave. Popé brought her alcohol and mescal, which intoxicated her. Indian women whipped her, because Linda had sex with their husbands, and they whipped John as well, who wanted to defend his mother. She once beat him because she did not want to be a mother and have a child but instantly kissed him. Thus Huxley describes Linda not only as a woman who is conditioned and therefore rejected by the Indians but also as a loving mother, which proves that her conditioning is not perfect. She is not able to adapt to the Indians' way of life, but never tried to return to the brave new world because she feels ashamed of having a baby.

John particularly remembers the happy time when he was told stories first by his mother about the nice music and games, the cleanliness and people's happiness of the "Other Place" and then by an old Indian about the creation of the world out of fog, about Mother Earth and Father Sky, Pookong and Jesus, etc. Though he could not understand everything, he loved the stories and thought about them a long time.

When Linda taught him to read by drawing pictures on the wall and writing sentences she knew from the "Other Place", John could read all the words his mother wrote after a short time. She then gave him the only book she had got as a Beta embryo-store worker. It was a practical instruction about embryo conditioning. Eventually John could read all the words but did not understand their meaning. Linda tried to answer his many questions for instance about chemicals but she was not able to explain anything properly. The old Indian's explanations of the creation of the world out of fog seemed to him much more comprehensible.

When John was twelve years old, Popé brought an old book he had found in a room the Indians used for ceremonies, *The Complete Works of William Shakespeare*. Though Linda thought that it was full of uncivilized nonsense, she believed that John could use it to practise his reading. The first quotation from *Hamlet* (III,4,91–94) seemed to him to describe the relationship between his mother and Popé: "[…] making love / Over the nasty sty" (p. 115). He was fascinated by the magic of Shakespeare's words that enabled him to express his hatred for Popé. He began to use Shakespeare's works to get into touch with strong feelings, to understand reality and to act more or less properly. Thus he felt urged to kill Popé when he read about Hamlet's thoughts of killing his uncle: "When he is drunk asleep, or in his rage / Or in the incestuous pleasure of his bed […]" (*Hamlet* III,3,89 f).
When John was fifteen, he enjoyed being taught to use clay to form different things by Mitsima, an old and wise Indian, who also wanted to teach him to make a bow. At the age of sixteen John fell in love with an Indian girl and was despairing when she married an Indian boy. As he was not allowed to take part in the initiation ceremonies of the young Indians, he felt rejected and lonely. Remembering the lines "Tomorrow and tomorrow and tomorrow" from *Macbeth* (V,5,18), which express the tyrant's tiredness of life, John even thought of committing suicide.
Bernard seems to understand John's strong feeling of loneliness, since he feels the same after being "decanted different", which John confirms by saying: "If one's different, one's bound to be lonely" (p. 120). John tells Bernard that he once wanted to feel like the crucified Jesus and stood with his arms out in the sun until he fell to the ground and severely hurt himself. But due to his conditioning Bernard is unable to feel pity for him but is horrified and disgusted when John wants to show him the scar on his head.
As Bernard is sure that the Director is John's father, he intends to take revenge on him and asks John to accompany him to London. When Bernard consents to John's wish that Linda should also be allowed to go with them, the two men are enthusiastic and John uses Miranda's words from Shakespeare's play *The Tempest* (V,1,182 f) for the first time in the novel to express his joy: "How many goodly creatures are there here! / How beauteous mankind is!" He mainly thinks of Lenina's beauty but interrupts himself when he says: "O brave new world" because he fears that she is married to Bernard. Bernard, however, neither knows who Miranda is nor what the word "married" means. John explains the meaning of the word and when Bernard denies being married to Lenina, John is happy and repeats Miranda's words "O brave new world that has such people in it!" But Bernard asks: "And, anyhow, hadn't you better wait till you actually see the new world?" (p. 112), one of the many examples of Huxley's irony that is supposed to contribute to the reader's critical approach to the brave new world.

Chapter Nine

As Lenina feels totally worn out after the horrifying experiences on the Reservation, she falls asleep in the rest-house for about 18 hours after having taken a high dose of soma, whereas Bernard flies to Santa Fé. There he rings up the Controller's office in Whitehall to ask permission for taking John and Linda to London. Mustapha Mond agrees because he considers it an interesting experiment and sends the necessary orders to the Warden of the Reservation. Meanwhile, John goes to the rest-house to see Bernard and starts weeping when he does not get an answer because he believes that Lenina and Bernard have left for London without him. But when he looks through the window of their apartment and sees Lenina's suitcase, he smashes the glass, climbs into the room, opens the suitcase and is enchanted by Lenina's perfumed underwear and clothes. When he hears a noise, he walks to the room where Lenina is sleeping. As he is enraptured by her beauty, he describes her by quoting from Shakespeare's plays *Troilus and Cressida* (I,1,54–58) and *Romeo and Juliet* (III,3,36–39). But contrary to Romeo, who touches Juliet's hand and kisses her though he first believed that he would profane Juliet with his "unworthiest hand" (I,5,92), John does not dare to touch Lenina and feels deeply ashamed when he desires to see her naked. Huxley uses irony again when John compares Juliet and Lenina and wrongly believes Lenina to be a virgin. The use of Shakespeare's words underlines that John is misled by them and fails to understand reality properly. When he hears the noise of Bernard's helicopter, he leaves the rest-house in panic to meet Bernard.

Chapter Ten

Before Bernard meets the Director after having returned to London, Huxley summarizes the production and conditioning of brave new world's in-vitro babies and again mentions the goals of hypnopaedia and the children's sex games. The Director intends to banish Bernard to Iceland in front of the high-caste workers because of Bernard's unorthodox behaviour that threatens to corrupt society and is more dangerous than murder because the dead can easily be replaced by producing additional embryos in the Hatchery.
When Bernard arrives, he conceals his nervousness behind his self-confidence. Huxley thus alludes to Bernard's secret plan mentioned before to raise suspense. The Director delivers a speech addressed to his Alpha workers and describes Bernard as an "enemy of Society" because of his "heretical views" and unorthodox behaviour referring to sport, soma, sex-life, etc. Finally, he tells the workers that Bernard is dismissed and banished to Iceland. But as soon as Linda enters the room she calls the Director Tomakin and thus reminds him of their former sexual relationship. She tells him that he is the father of her son, who is then called in by Bernard. When John shouts "My father!" the Alpha workers start laughing loudly about all the "pornographic" words used by Linda and John, such as baby, mother, father. Meanwhile, the

Director has totally lost his self-confidence and as he feels ashamed and humiliated, he flees out of the Fertilizing Room.

Chapter Eleven

Whereas all the upper-caste people want to see John, they are not at all interested in seeing Linda, since she is no real savage but a conditioned Beta and as a mother she is an obscenity and looks repulsive due to her old and dirty appearance. Linda, too, does not wish to see anybody and takes ever larger doses of soma. The doctor knows that she shortens her life but as it is not possible to stop getting old, he thinks that her death is "a good thing". Moreover, he believes that taking soma is "a bit of what our ancestors used to call eternity" (p. 135). John murmurs the line "Eternity was in our lips and eyes" from Shakespeare's *Antony and Cleopatra* (I,3,35), which seems to help him understand the doctor's words. But when the doctor insinuates that people who haven't got to do any useful work in the brave new world are useless and should die John protests though he is not able to change Linda, who lives in a world of hallucinations. The doctor, however, is grateful for having had the opportunity to see an "example of senility in a human being" (p. 136).

As everybody wants to meet John and Bernard who arranges everything as his guardian, he feels important for the first time in his life since all the people who did not like him before are now polite to him and offer presents. He is invited to parties by the most dignified representatives of the World State. He boasts of having all the girls he wants and no longer feels an outsider. But as he also criticizes the order of the society, which makes him feel even more important, people talk about him behind his back and predict his fall.

Bernard shows John around to see every technical invention of the brave new world but is disappointed because the Savage is not really astonished. When John is told that the speed of the Bombay Green Rocket is 1250 kilometres an hour, he only thinks of the airy spirit Ariel in Shakespeare's *The Tempest*, who is by far faster (cf. p. 138). Bernard informs the Controller about John's behaviour and views in a report and admits that he agrees with the Savage, who finds the brave new world infantile. Mustapha Mond dislikes Bernard's lecturing him and decides to give him a lesson.

John is shown a factory of lighting-sets for helicopters where numerous different low-caste workers are busily producing different parts, which are transported on an assembly line and then fit together to mechanisms that are controlled, packed in crates and loaded in lorries. Whereas the manager is extremely proud of the factory, the Savage is shocked and uses Miranda's words "O brave new world that has such people in it" ironically. Then he rushes out and begins to vomit.

In his next report to the Controller Bernard writes that John does not take soma, frequently visits his mother and shows strong feelings of distress and

attachment, which in the brave world have been suppressed by the early conditioning of children.
At Eton College, which is an ensemble of concrete high-rise buildings with a steel statue of Our Ford in the centre (cf. the picture on p. 122), Bernard and John are welcomed by the provost and the head mistress. The school is only for upper-caste boys and girls. While Bernard successfully makes advances to the head mistress, the provost opens several classroom doors. The most intelligent pupils are studying elementary relativity. But when John asks Bernard what that is, he tries to explain it, but eventually gives up and goes to the geography room. There Beta-Minuses are informed about the primitive life on a savage reservation, which is not worth civilizing. The pupils are shown a film about a group of pueblo Indians, the crucified Jesus and the eagle image of Pookong. When the Indians confess their sins and whip themselves, the pupils start laughing. John is annoyed and confused and wants to know why everybody is laughing but the provost only replies that it is "so extraordinarily funny" (p. 142). In the Hypnopaedic Control Room the hypnopaedic lessons are printed. When they pass the school library and the head mistress denies John's question whether they also read Shakespeare, the provost tells him that there are only reference books in the school library. Instead of reading literature, the pupils are expected to go to the feelies if they want to be entertained. When Bernard and John are leaving, five buses full of boys and girls are returning from the death-conditioning lesson at Slough Crematorium. Bernard interrupts their flight back to London at the Television Corporation factory to ring up Lenina while John observes the nearly identically looking lower-caste workers after their shift. They are queuing in front of the monorail station to get their ration of soma.
To her great joy, Bernard has asked Lenina on the phone to go to the feelies with John. As she knows the Savage, she has also become famous and is invited by several celebrities of the brave new world, even by the Arch-Community-Songster of Canterbury, who all want to know what it is like to have sex with the Savage. But as she likes John very much and he seems to avoid her, she feels miserable. In the cinema the synthetic music, the perfumes from the scent organs and the technically produced sensations irritate John, who is disgusted at the primitive adventurous sex film about a black man and a Beta blonde. Though he desires Lenina, he feels ashamed of his desire and leaves her abruptly, which Lenina is unable to understand since she wants to have sex with him. In his room John begins to read Shakespeare's *Othello*, because like in the film the protagonist in Shakespeare's play is a black man. Meanwhile Lenina takes soma to overcome her frustration.

Chapter Twelve

Though Bernard has invited several celebrities of the brave new world to meet John, the Savage refuses to leave his room despite Bernard's urgent pleas and expresses his contempt of the Arch-Community-Songster of Canterbury in Zuñi. When Bernard informs the guests about John's refusal, they are furious and regret that they pretended to respect Bernard and treated him politely only to meet the Savage. In fact, they despise him because of his unorthodox behaviour. Lenina is deeply disappointed and is no longer sure that John really likes her. The guests, who begin to gossip about Bernard's insufficient height and that he was nearly banished to Iceland, ignore him. Finally, the Arch-Community-Songster warns Bernard, who has totally lost his self-confidence, and orders Lenina to follow him, obviously to have sex with him. When all the guests have left, Bernard despairs and takes a high dose of soma.

Meanwhile, John has been reading *Romeo and Juliet*, whereas Mustapha Mond has finished studying a paper about a new theory of biology. Though he admires the "masterly piece of work", he forbids publishing it and orders the author to be put under supervision, because it might recondition the higher castes. They might question the present social order and believe that the purpose of life is not well-being but the enlargement of knowledge (cf. pp. 154 f). Though the Controller agrees and does not seem to identify with the goals of the brave new world, he nevertheless does everything to preserve them.

While John is fascinated by the magic of Romeo's admiration of Juliet's beauty (cf. *Romeo and Juliet* I,5,43–46) and the Arch-Community-Songster goes to bed with Lenina, Bernard is lost in the dream world of a soma "paradise" (p. 156). The next morning the Savage tells Bernard that he would prefer being "unhappy than have the sort of false, lying happiness" people have in the brave new world (cf. p. 156). Though Bernard knows that the Savage is right, he is mischievous and wants to take revenge on John for not having come to the party. He also intends to "take some revenge on Helmholtz for his generosity"(p. 157) of renewing their friendship after Bernard's cutting him dead when he was considered important as John's guardian.

But in the meantime also Helmholtz has come into difficulties because he gave his students a poem about loneliness he had written himself, which endangers the conditioning through hypnopaedic slogans. Helmholtz, however, is really happy because he believes to have discovered his creativity, which is also the reason why he and the Savage spontaneously become friends. Helmholtz is fascinated by John's reading some lines from Shakespeare's allegorical poem *The Phoenix and the Turtle*, and when he listens to the lovers' first dialogues in *Romeo and Juliet*, he is delighted and admits that Shakespeare "makes our best propaganda technicians look absolutely silly" (p. 160). But nevertheless, he is not able to overcome his conditioning because he finds Romeo's and Juliet's passionate love and her refusal to marry Paris without telling her parents that she is already married ridiculous. Finally, he explodes with laughter when John recites Juliet's imploring words "Is there no pity [sitting] in the clouds / That sees into the bottom of my grief? / O sweet my mother, cast me not away! [...]" (III,5,196–198), since he finds the words 'mother' and 'father' obscene. Moreover, he thinks it stupid not to burn the body of Juliet's cousin Tybalt to produce phosphorus. As also Bernard has frequently laughed about the tragedy, John feels hurt and locks the book away. Finally, Helmholtz "explains" why Shakespeare was such a "marvellous propaganda technician": Because he could write about so many insane and painful themes (cf. p. 161). They should be replaced by "some other kind of madness and violence" (p. 162). Helmholtz is dissatisfied with his own propaganda work but does not at all know what he should write about instead.

Chapter Thirteen

Lenina does not tell Henry Foster, who thinks that she is sick, why she looks dejected and sad. As she only thinks of John, she forgets to vaccinate one of the Alpha Minus babies against the sleeping sickness and is thus responsible for his death several years later. When she tells Fanny that the Savage is the only man she really wants, her friend advises her not to wait for him but take the initiative. She takes soma to make herself forget her fears and goes to see John, who falls on his knees, kisses her hand and expresses his admiration of Lenina's beauty by reciting some of Ferdinand's words about Miranda from Shakespeare's *The Tempest* (III,1,7 ff). As he feels unworthy of Lenina, he wants to give her a present or do something for her as a sign of his love, which Lenina is conditioned to think unnecessary. When John mentions that in Malpais and also in Shakespeare's plays people marry, Lenina is shocked and does not understand his quotations from Shakespeare's plays. But when he tells her that he loves her "more than anything in the world" (p. 167), she embraces and kisses him. Instantly, John shrinks back because he does not want to turn his love into lust, which Lenina cannot understand. She begins to undress and expresses her feelings by quoting several hypnopaedic slogans such as "Hug me till you drug me, honey" (p. 169), until John gets furious, calls her a whore and pushes her away. Quoting from Shakespeare's *King Lear* and *Othello*, he insults and threatens Lenina, who is terribly frightened and escapes when John leaves the flat because he is informed on the telephone that his mother is seriously ill.

Chapter Fourteen

When John reaches the high-rise hospital for dying people, he sees a long line of colourful helicopters used to transport the diseased to Slough Crematorium. Linda lies in one of the twenty beds in a bright room filled with gay synthetic music and regularly changing perfumes. Television is on throughout the day. The nurse is shocked when John uses the word "mother" and is unable to understand John's grief when she tells him that Linda will die and that there is no hope. When John passes the beds of the other dying people he shudders because they still look young. Linda is half watching a tennis match on TV, half dozing. After recognizing her son she suddenly falls asleep while John remembers his childhood in Malpais with her and begins to weep. They are disturbed by a noisy group of Delta children who are supposed to get their lesson in death-conditioning. Linda is alarmed when some of the children express their disgust because they see a really old woman of forty-four contrary to all the other sixty-year-old women in their "second infancy". John beats one of the curious children and is warned by the nurse to be thrown out if he spoils their death-conditioning. He continues to remember both the fearful experiences and his mother's love on the Reservation while Linda dreams of Popé. When she seems to mistake John for Popé, the Savage is angry and shakes her to make her recognize him. But her eyes are filled with terror and she dies. John feels guilty of her death, mourns her and is inconsolable. The nurse is upset about his indecent behaviour since he endangers the children's death-conditioning. When several children eating chocolate stand grinning around Linda's bed and ask John if she is dead, he leaves the room in silence.

Chapter Fifteen

When John sees the menial staff of the hospital for the dying, all of them repulsive twins, he realizes that his former view of the people of the brave new world is wrong. Again he is reminded of Miranda's words in Shakespeare's *The Tempest* (cf. p. 183). But this time he is not deluded to apply Shakespeare's words inadequately but recognizes that the knowledge of Shakespeare helps him to understand the brave new world properly as a nightmare. He is fully aware now of his mother having been a slave and ruined by soma. When the Delta workers desire to get their daily ration of soma after work, John tries to liberate them from their drug addiction and to stop the distribution of that "poison to soul as well as body" (p. 184), but in vain. When he begins to throw the soma pills out of the window, the Delta workers are furious. Meanwhile, Bernard and Helmholtz have arrived and want to rescue John when the spraying of soma by the police and a "Voice of Good Feeling" from the synthetic music box appease the crowd. After the Delta workers have got their soma ration, Bernard, Helmholtz and John are arrested and taken to a police car.

Chapter Sixteen

In the Controller's study John discovers Ford's biography, reads some sentences but finds them uninteresting. When the Controller enters, John expresses his dislike of the brave new world. But when John says that he likes the "music in the air" and refers to Shakespeare's *The Tempest*, the Controller delights and tells that he has also read Shakespeare's plays though the dramatist's works are prohibited like all things that are old. He declares: "But as I make the laws here, I can also break them" (p. 190). Though he agrees with John that Shakespeare's plays are beautiful, he points out that in the brave new world people are conditioned only to like new things. He also rejects John's idea of writing "something new that's like *Othello*" and can be understood by the people. Whereas Bernard is afraid of saying anything critical, Helmholtz supports John's argument and confirms that he would like to write a new *Othello* but the Controller replies that he will never write such a play. Moreover, nobody would understand it since the brave new world is totally different from Othello's world. As it is impossible to make planes without steel it is also impossible to write tragedies in a world of social stability. In the brave new world everybody is happy because the world is stable. People only want what they are conditioned to want. They live a safe, healthy, passionless life without any family troubles or the fear of death and can take soma whenever necessary. The Controller laughs at John because he tried to liberate the Delta workers from taking the drug though they are unable to understand the word "liberty".

When John underlines that *Othello* is a good play, the Controller says that in the brave new world high art had to be sacrificed for stability. Instead, people enjoy the agreeable feelings produced by the feelies and the scent organ. To John, such things are stupid, which he underlines by referring to an image in *Macbeth* (V,5,26), which is used there by the protagonist to stress the absurdity of his life: "told by an idiot" (p. 191). Helmholtz again supports John's view because he has recognized that as an Emotional Engineer he is expected to write though "there's nothing to say". Mustapha Mond, however, compares writing about pure sensations with producing planes out of an extremely small amount of steel, which is a great achievement. He underlines that agreeable feelings contribute to people's "happiness" and stability, which is, of course, less spectacular than instability, passion and misery.

When John asks the Controller why there are such a lot of primitive, ugly and identically looking people in the brave new world, Mustapha Mond replies that such people are useful and the basis of society. If only Alphas were produced, they would destabilize society since they are individuals who are conditioned to make a free choice within certain limits and would protest against doing the primitive work of the lower castes. To prove the correctness of his view, the Controller describes the failure of the Cyprus experiment when only Alphas were allowed to live on the island and were incapable of working as farmers or industrial workers. The Alpha society finally collapsed because of unrest, strikes and a civil war.

Stability can only be achieved if the population consists of only ten percent Alphas and the rest of lower castes that like their work, entertainment, sex and soma. Their work could be reduced to three or four working hours a day but an experiment in Ireland has shown that the people did not know what to do in their leisure time and took more soma. As every change endangers stability, people in the brave new world also continue to work on farms since it takes more time to produce food agriculturally than industrially which would be no problem to do. Like art also science is dangerous because every new invention can destabilize society. Mond explains that he once was a scientist who was not interested in orthodox theories but in real science and tried to discover something new. When he mentions that that was the reason why he was nearly banished to an island, which will soon happen to Bernard and Helmholtz, Bernard loses his nerve and pleadingly asks the Controller not to send him to Iceland because, contrary to Helmholtz and John, he did not do anything wrong. As he is not able to calm down, he is carried out by three men and given "a good soma vaporization" (p. 196). Mond cannot understand Bernard's fear since living on an island is no punishment but a reward because it means to meet interesting and intelligent people, real individuals.

When Helmholtz asks Mond why he does not go there, the Controller regretfully admits that he had the choice to be sent to an island or to become one of the ten World Controllers. He decided to give up pure science and "to serve happiness. Other people's – not mine" (p. 198).

He did it out of duty because real science and truth are dangerous for society. They were considered the supreme values until Our Ford began to lay more stress on comfort and happiness through mass production. As there is no sense in talking about science and truth when everything is destroyed, people changed their minds after the Nine Years' War. Since then everybody lives in peace and science is controlled and restricted.

Mond points out that unorthodox people need not be executed any more but are sent to one of the many islands. When he asks Helmholtz which of the islands he would prefer, Helmholtz wishes to go to an island with a bad climate because that would be better for a writer. The Controller expresses that he likes Helmholtz's views very much though officially he must reject them and suggests that he should go to the Falkland Islands. Helmholtz agrees and leaves to look after Bernard.

Chapter Seventeen

Like art and science also religion was given up after the Nine Years' War. John would like to talk about God, solitude and death, but he does not know how to express his ideas since even Shakespeare is no help. The Controller opens a large safe and takes out *The Holy Bible* and several other religious and philosophical books. John tries to understand what the Controller is talking about by reciting lines from Shakespeare's *King John* and *Hamlet*. Mustapha Mond reads out passages from a book by Cardinal Newman and the French statesman and philosopher Maine de Biran, who point out that man becomes more religious the older he grows because he no longer believes that he is independent and strong as he thought when he was young. Growing old he

needs the support of something reliable, "an absolute and everlasting truth" (p. 201). Mond, however, points out that the old philosophers are wrong since they did not imagine a future world where everybody is happy, which has been realized in the present World State. Now people live in prosperity and enjoy their youthful desires as long as they live and think that God does not exist. In a highly civilized and technical society controlled by man God is useless. When John asks him if it is not natural to believe in God when you feel lonely and think about death, the Controller replies that the people in the brave new world are conditioned to hate loneliness and always live in a community.
When John recites some lines from *King Lear* (V,3,171–175) to underline that God is just and calls man to account for his vices, Mond tells him that in the modern society people can enjoy pleasant vices without the fear of punishment. He states: "You can't have a lasting civilization without plenty of pleasant vices" (p. 203). But John insists on the idea that "God's the reason for everything noble and fine and heroic" as he knows it from the Reservation. Mond, however, tells him that in a society without wars you do not need nobility and heroism. Everyone is conditioned to do what he ought to. In case anything unpleasant happens, you take soma, which is "Christianity without tears" (p. 205). Once more the Savage recites lines from *Othello* and *Hamlet* and gives an example of a young Indian's love to a girl in order to prove that it is worthwhile to learn to overcome problems and dangers. But Mond tells him that one condition of perfect health in the brave new world is to stimulate fears and rage artificially from time to time by a compulsory Violent Passion Surrogate treatment, which replaces the experience of real passions.
When John finally underlines that he does not want to live without God, poetry, real danger, freedom, goodness and sin and insists on his right to be unhappy, feel pain, get sick and old, the Controller runs out of arguments and shrugs his shoulders.

Chapter Eighteen

When Helmholtz and Bernard want to say good-bye to John, who looks pale and sick, John tells them that civilization has poisoned him. He would like to go to the islands with his friends but the Controller does not allow it because he wants to continue the experiment with him. But John has decided to live alone in an abandoned air-lighthouse in Surrey, where he spends the first night praying to God, Jesus and the Indian gods. He enjoys the beauty and loneliness of the landscape around and decides to become independent from society by growing fruit and vegetables in his garden and hunt animals with a bow. As he wishes to be purified from civilization and his sins, he begins to whip himself like the Indians on the Reservation. But as his self-punishment has been observed by three Delta-Minus land-workers, a reporter of the upper-caste paper *The Hourly Radio* arrives to interview him. Instead of telling

him anything, he shouts at the reporter in his Indian language and kicks him hard. When more reporters arrive, they are also threatened and driven away by the Savage.
As John has promised to forget Lenina but is not able to do so, he again whips himself, which is filmed by a feely expert living in John's neighbourhood. As soon as the film is shown, a lot of helicopters arrive filled with curious people who want to see John whipping himself. When Lenina also arrives in a helicopter, John turns pale, calls her a strumpet and slashes her and himself with his whip like mad while the crowd is delighted and starts singing and dancing until they beat each other in an orgy, in which also the Savage takes part.
The next morning, after a soma sleep, the Savage is exhausted, feels deep remorse and despairs. When in the evening a crowd of people arrive who read about the orgy in the papers, they find John dead. He has hanged himself.

The Characters

Most of the characters in Huxley's dystopian novel represent the brave new world either as main characters such as Mustapha Mond, Bernard Marx and Lenina Crowne or more or less minor characters such as Henry Foster and Fanny Crowne. They are confronted with John the Savage, who grew up on an Indian Reservation and seems to be the protagonist in the second half of the novel. Also the minor characters promote the action to a certain extent or serve to partly understand it, for instance John's mother Linda and the Warden of the Reservation. Whereas the characters with individual names belong to the upper castes, the vast majority of this future society consists of the anonymous lower-caste masses that are necessary to keep the brave new world stable by their low or even lacking intelligence and inferior work.

Mustapha Mond

As the Resident World Controller of Western Europe, Mustapha Mond is one of the ten World Controllers and the most powerful man in the brave new world. The Controller sees to it that the inhabitants think and act according to the principles of this future society: Community, Identity, Stability.
Whereas the Director of the Central London Hatchery and Conditioning Centre describes the technical and biochemical production and conditioning of human beings and gives some background information, Mustapha Mond is able to outline the ideology of the brave new world and explain in detail why the total manipulation of man is considered necessary. Before he appears in Chapter Three, the Director already underlines that the Controllers make

the laws everybody has to respect (cf. p. 31), and when Mustapha Mond arrives, he is enthusiastically welcomed by the Director and saluted respectfully by the students. By quoting Ford, Mond tells them that history is nonsense. As in the brave new world it is useless to know anything about ancient cultures, old literature, philosophy and music, the students are not taught history at all. The Director gets confused when Mond by referring to the rumours that he owns forbidden books such as the Bible and poetry only says that he does not want to corrupt them.
Moreover, the Controller explains why family life has been abolished in the brave new world. In former times living in a family meant living in prison-like dirty rooms together with a father, a frequently pregnant mother and a lot of brothers and sisters. There were conflicts and difficult emotional relationships. Since the larger family also consisted of all kinds of other relatives such as uncles and aunts, life was "full of madness and suicide" (p. 39). Contrary to monogamy, love and exclusive relationships in former times, people in the brave new world live according to the hypnopaedic slogan: "Everyone belongs to everyone else." Because of their inability to feel strong passions and their ability to take things easy, the world has become stable. As civilization is based on social stability and social stability on individual stability (cf. p. 42), stability is the most important goal of the brave new world. That is why people are industrially produced and conditioned to make their lives easy and make them content with their work. That is also the reason why Christianity, Parliament and liberty have been abolished. In the modern society such things are unnecessary since men are physically and chemically equal now.
As after the Nine Years' War and the great Economic Collapse there was no alternative but to decide between destruction and world control, the decision was to establish a totally controlled World State. At first the World Controllers used force to subdue and kill people who did not adapt to the new world order but for instance went on admiring art. But then they realized that people could be totally brought under control with the help of biochemistry, conditioning and sleep-teaching. Since then people have been conditioned to like their work and enjoy the permanent consumption of sex, sports and other kinds of entertainment. Instead of the Christian God they believe in Our Ford and take soma, the perfect drug without side effects, whenever they feel bad. They do not get or feel old since they look young and enjoy sex, work, consumption and other distractions until they die without fear at the age of 60.
At the end of Chapter Three when the Director shuns away two little children playing sex games, the Controller says: "Poor little children", which sounds ambiguous. He might feel sorry for them because they are driven away or even regret to a certain extent that they are not able to play other games.
In the following seven chapters Mustapha Mond is only mentioned when he

allows Bernard and Lenina to visit the Reservation and gives permission to take the Savage and his mother to the brave new world since it is "of sufficient scientific interest" (p. 123). He reads Bernard's reports about John and Linda, in which Bernard mentions that John is not fascinated by the technological inventions of the modern state and insists on believing in the existence of the human soul. But Mond is not very much interested in such information. When Bernard underlines that he agrees with John's dislike of the "civilized infantility" of the brave new world and tries to direct the Controller's attention to that problem, Mond gets angry and decides to teach Bernard a lesson, because he feels school-mastered by him (cf. p. 138).

Mond, who is interested in scientific books, is fascinated by a new biological theory. But he believes that it would endanger the stability of the modern world since it might recondition the upper castes to believe that the purpose of life is not well-being but the enlargement of knowledge (cf. pp. 155 f). That is why he forbids publishing it and considers whether the author should be sent to the island of St Helena. Thus Mond believes that it is his duty to stop scientific progress if it might be a danger to the brave new world. When he admits that it would be great fun to him not to think about "happiness" (cf. p. 155), i.e. people's pleasure and comfort, he seems to be discontent with his position of a Controller and does not really identify with the principles of the brave new world.

Though old books such as Shakespeare's works are prohibited in the brave new world Mustapha Mond owns them. He has read them and finds them beautiful. His unrestricted power is stressed when he states: "But as I make the laws here, I can also break them" (p. 190) without being punished. He thus underlines his arbitrary rule and that everybody including Bernard is controlled by him. Whereas the inhabitants of the modern state are conditioned according to the principles of identity, community and stability, Mustapha Mond can personally violate these principles since he is an extraordinarily intelligent Alpha Plus, lives on his own as an "individual", and is an arbitrary and cynical despot.

As the vast majority of the modern world's inhabitants are unable to understand the old books, in particular Shakespeare's plays, because they are conditioned to be infantile, Helmholtz, who is also an individual to a certain extent, is unable to understand the conflict between Juliet and her parents when the Savage recites the girl's grief from Shakespeare's tragedy. Nevertheless, Helmholtz wishes to write something worth writing about but the Controller tells him that that will never be since tragedies can only be written if there is social instability, which is not given in the brave new world where people "get what they want, and never want what they can't get" (pp. 191 f). They are "so conditioned that they practically can't help behaving as they ought to behave" (p. 191). Mond admits that Shakespeare's plays are good and better than the feelies, but the high art had to be sacrificed to achieve stability. Instead, there are the feelies and the scent organ which "mean a lot of agreeable sensations to the audience" (p. 191). Helmholtz, who produces such films, disqualifies them as "idiotic" since it means "writing when there is nothing to say". Mond agrees but he seems to contradict himself or to misunderstand art when he points out that it affords "enormous ingenuity" to produce "works of art out of practically nothing but pure sensation" (p. 192).

Mond also underlines that modern society cannot do without the rather stupid lower-caste workers since they are "the foundation on which everything else is built" (p. 192). A society of Alphas would end in chaos as proved by an experiment on Cyprus many years ago when they denied to do simple work, organized strikes, were ambitious and began a civil war. That is why the society of brave new world only consists of 10 % Alphas but of 90 % lower-caste inhabitants who enjoy their work and also the long working hours since they do not know what to do in an additional spare time. Again Mond justifies his decision by referring to an experiment in Ireland that proved that more leisure only meant unrest and a higher consumption of soma.

Though the Controller seems to believe in the validity of scientifically well-founded experiments, he underlines that pure science is dangerous because every discovery might contribute to change and endanger stability. Before he became a Controller, he had been a gifted scientist, who questioned orthodox theory and according to "real science" wanted to discover something new. That is why he was nearly banished to an island where he could have met the most intelligent people. But he decided out of duty to become a Controller, though he sometimes regrets this decision, because he is interested in truth and knows that conditioning people to feel happy means betraying them. He points out that Ford had already contributed to the shift "from truth and beauty to comfort and happiness by introducing mass production" (p. 197), and after the Nine Years' War science had been restricted to what is of immediate interest. Asking innovative questions has been discouraged to guarantee the stability of the modern world.

Mond is a split character, who openly admits that he is interested in truth and knowledge, appreciates poetry and admires Helmholtz' wish to become a creative writer but at the same time suppresses people's individuality, family life, real science, thirst for knowledge and art in the name of a false happiness. That is why he also feels relieved that instead of executing people like Helmholtz and Bernard, his position of a Controller allows him to banish them to one of the many islands. To a certain extent, he is characterized by Huxley as a tragic figure who seems to have come to the wrong decision of doing his "duty" to guarantee social stability though he still loves truth and beauty and envies the people he banishes.

Apart from scientific books and literature the Controller also owns and reads the Bible and other religious and philosophical works, which are prohibited.

He seems to be convinced that in a highly civilized, technological modern society God is useless because people are prosperous and "happy". They are conditioned to live in a community and never feel lonely. They do not fear death and need not be heroic since there are no wars any more. If they need to feel passions such as fear and fury, they can be cured by artificial stimulation from time to time, and if something unpleasant happens, they can take soma to feel well again and forget pain and trouble. But Mond is unable to convince the Savage of the uselessness of God, poetry, freedom, ethical values and the experience of unhappiness and old age. He cynically states that "you can't have a lasting civilization without plenty of pleasant vices" (p. 204). He seems to be aware of the loss of the true sense of life in the brave new world but is not willing to admit it officially. Finally, he runs out of arguments and shrugs his shoulders.
To sum up, Mustapha Mond controls the dystopian society that must function like a machine that will never stop or break down. People are considered replacement parts that keep the social machinery permanently going. If they do not fit in like Helmholtz and Bernard they are removed. The Controller himself deliberately breaks the laws that all the inhabitants of the brave new world have to obey. Contrary to the Alphas, the lower castes are even unable to break them since they are totally conditioned to be pleased with their specialized roles in society and have no idea of an alternative life. Mond knows that men might experience true happiness for instance through science, art and literature but by their biochemical production and conditioning Mond cynically makes them unable to live a human life of happiness and pain and die with dignity.

The Director

The Director of the Central London Hatchery and Conditioning Centre is the first character Huxley describes in his novel. He is introduced as a competent and well-instructed expert who is conscious of his superior status and expects to be respected by everybody. When he conducts a group of male students around the Hatchery and Conditioning Centre from the Fertilizing Room to the Bottling Room, the Social Predestination Room and the Embryo Store to the Decanting Room, he uses a lot of technical terms such as Bokanovsky's Process and Podsnap's Technique. The students hardly understand his descriptions and explanations but quickly scribble them down in their notebooks rather automatically. The Director feels enthusiastic about the high standard of his factory and the workers' skill to produce the different caste members and for example heat-resistant specialists for tropical work or engineers who are conditioned to repair rockets without feeling dizzy. He identifies with his work and is ambitious because he intends to accelerate the ripening process of mature eggs.

The students admire the production process of embryos uncritically and do not dare to ask questions that might help them grasp the Director's lectures better. When one of the students is "fool enough to ask" what the advantage is to produce scores of identical twins, the Director intimidates him by saying: "Can't you see?" (p. 11). Sometimes Huxley cracks a joke, for instance when the Director tells the students that the embryos that are conditioned by constant rotation to become rocket-plane engineers are "only happy when they're standing on their heads" (p. 20).

The Director also informs the students about experiments in foreign Hatcheries that failed, e.g. the production of individuals who are sexually and intellectually mature at a very early age. He gives the reason why the inhabitants of the brave new world are not naturally born but industrially produced. Everything is done to produce and condition people who will be content and happy with what they are destined to be and thus guarantee social stability.

When the Director leads the students to the Neo-Pavlovian Conditioning Rooms and asks them to observe everything intensely, he explains how the babies are conditioned to hate books and nature and consume sports and the means of transportation. He finally triumphantly states: "What man has joined, nature is powerless to put asunder" (p. 23). Though historical knowledge is considered useless and the Director underlines that "most historical facts are unpleasant" (p. 25), he informs the students about the discovery of hypnopaedia in Poland during Ford's lifetime and also uses "obscene" words like mother and father that irritate and confuse the boys. He praises hypnopaedia as the best method of moral education since the children are intensively influenced to behave according to the hypnopaedic slogans as long as they live.

Though the Director appears to be a perfect expert who identifies with his work, he is driven by his guilty conscience to tell Bernard about his visit to the Reservation as a young man with his girl Linda and his return without her since she got lost there, which still haunts him in his dreams. Obviously, the Director's feelings towards Linda were stronger than allowed in the brave new world. When he recognizes his mistake of having told something personal to his subordinate, he tries to play the "trivial anecdote" down, criticizes Bernard's "unorthodox" behaviour and threatens to banish him to Iceland. The Director is unfair since he vents his anger on Bernard and misuses his superior position. But Bernard takes revenge on him by confronting him with Linda, who calls him by his pet name Tomakin, and his son John. As he is thus exposed as a hypocrite who manipulates people to live according to the principles of the brave new world but has severely violated them himself, the Director runs off like a coward and finally resigns.

Bernard Marx

Bernard Marx, an Alpha-Plus psychologist, seems to be the protagonist in the novel until the Savage becomes more and more important for the action and the elucidation of Huxley's implicit or explicit criticism of the dystopian society. The first time when Bernard appears at the beginning of the novel, Henry Foster, a scientist in the London Hatchery, and the Assistant Director of Predestination show their dislike and disrespect of him when they see him in the lift going up to the changing rooms. The reader learns that Bernard is mentally and physically different from other Alphas since he seems to be in a mood of melancholy and disdains his colleagues when they talk about a stupid film or about Lenina Crowne as if she were only good for sex.
Bernard is described by Lenina's friend Fanny as ugly because for an Alpha he is too small and looks like a Gamma-Minus (cf. p. 152). She assumes that he got alcohol into his blood-surrogate by mistake when he was an embryo. Nevertheless, Lenina Crowne likes Bernard but he is too shy to confess that he likes her too. When she directly asks him to have sex with her, he is confused and does not want to talk about it in public. On the other hand, Bernard envies his friend Helmholtz Watson, who is extremely popular with girls, and hypocritically agrees when Helmholtz tells him that he is annoyed at being idolized by them.
Though Lenina finds him odd, she decides to take the opportunity to accompany him to the Reservation since as an Alpha-Plus psychologist Bernard belongs to the small group of people who are allowed to go there. But whereas Bernard would like to be alone with her and go for a walk in the Lake District, Lenina persuades him against his will to join a crowd watching a wrestling championship. On their way back to London, Bernard tells her that he would like to be himself and not "a cell in the social body" and that he wishes to be free and not enslaved by his conditioning. Lenina, who doesn't know better than to repeat hypnopaedic slogans, does not understand him at all and is terribly shocked by his "blasphemy" (cf. p. 83). When he takes soma and has sex with her, Bernard feels miserable and remorseful because he considers his behaviour infantile.
Bernhard's behaviour deviates from the other Alphas since he does not totally follow the hypnopaedic slogans such as "Everyone belongs to everyone else" but rejects promiscuity and also refuses to take soma sometimes to overcome his sullenness or melancholy mood. When he takes part in the Solidarity Service, which serves to strengthen the sense of community, he does not feel the Coming of the Greater Being though he had to take soma tablets. Instead, he feels even more separate and isolated. As he looks like a Gamma he dislikes himself: "I am I, and I wish I wasn't" (p. 61), is mocked at by women, not respected by the lower castes and feels an outsider in the brave new world. He envies his Alpha colleagues Henry Foster and Benito

Hoover, who are totally integrated into the modern society, whereas his friend Helmholtz Watson wishes that he should feel pride instead of self-pity and would not be boastful if he felt sure, for instance when he believes that the Director will not carry out the threat to send him to Iceland.
On the Reservation Bernard pretends not to be moved by the primitive living conditions and the cruel ceremonies whereas Lenina is shocked and wants to leave. Contrary to the hypnopaedic lessons, he even wishes that Lenina should experience motherhood. When he presumes that John the Savage is the Director's son and Linda his girl who got lost, he decides to take revenge on his superior by taking them to London and confronting them with the Director. In London he shows John around and visits a factory and Eton College but the Savage dislikes everything, which Bernard informs the Controller about in his regular reports.
As he is John's guardian and everybody wants to meet the Savage and invites them to parties, Bernard feels very important now and no longer an outsider in the brave new world. But when the Savage refuses to see anybody and thus disappoints Bernard and upsets the important persons he invited to a party, Bernard is blamed and despised by them again. He takes soma to forget the disgrace and humiliation. But as he feels miserable the next morning and is treated like a friend by the Savage and Helmholtz, he maliciously plans to take some revenge on them.
Bernard is envious when he realizes that Helmholtz and the Savage immediately become friends because Helmholtz is to a certain extent fascinated by Shakespeare's poetry. He is pleased when he learns that his best friend Helmholtz has also come into conflict with the Controller because of giving his "unorthodox" poem about solitude to his students.
Bernard behaves like a coward when John is attacked by Delta workers and does not defend him but cries for help and tries to escape when they are arrested by the police. As he is so stupid to schoolmaster Mustapha Mond in one of his reports about the Savage, the Controller decides to send him to an island and when Bernard realizes that he must go to Iceland, he again behaves like a coward, pins the blame on his friends, tries to flee and is carried out of the room by force.
Bernard is a rather complex and inconsistent character with positive and negative traits. He changes from an outcast to a self-assured person who is only respected in the brave new world as long as he is the guardian of the Savage. As he has not been perfectly conditioned by mistake, he is an individual, who endangers society's conformity and stability and is banished to an island against his will.

Lenina and Fanny Crowne

Lenina Crowne, a Beta vaccination worker at the Central London Hatchery and Conditioning Centre, is described as "uncommonly pretty" when she is mentioned for the first time. She is the most desirable woman in the brave new world who had already sex with nearly everyone. She vaccinates embryos against typhoid and sleeping sickness without making mistakes except once later on when she feels miserable because John the Savage does not seem to like her. She is used to be an object of desire even of the Arch-Community-Songster and behaves promiscuously according to her hypnopaedic conditioning. She always dresses attractively, uses different perfumes and wears a beautiful Malthusian belt that prevents conception. But she is not really loved by anybody but considered "pneumatic" and looked upon as "a bit of meat" (p. 45), which she does not mind to be (cf. p. 84).
Despite her promiscuous behaviour she remains "faithful" to Henry Foster for four months, which is criticized by her friend Fanny as too long since it is against the hypnopaedic rule that everyone belongs to everyone else. Lenina likes Bernard and makes advances to him though he is too small for an Alpha-Plus and looks sullen and is in a melancholy mood. She might feel sympathy or pity for him, which would mean a deviation of her conditioning. On the other hand, she is curious and wants to seize the opportunity to accompany him to the Reservation. As soon as she meets John she likes him, but cannot understand why he expects her to be like Shakespeare's Juliet. But her emotions are stronger than usual, so she admits that she likes him "more than anybody I've ever known" (p. 152). This is the reason why she is terrified when John refuses to have sex with her and cruelly beats her. At the end of the novel when she wants to meet the Savage again she despairs because John calls her a whore and whips her terribly.
On the Reservation she is horrified by the dirty surroundings, the Indians' primitive life, marriage and natural birth, their cruel religious ceremonies, Linda's old age, etc and finally takes soma to forget everything. When Bernard tells her that he would like to be free and not socially conditioned, Lenina is shocked by such a blasphemous view. In all the situations that seem unbearable and shocking to her she tries to help herself by quoting hypnopaedic slogans or taking soma.

Fanny Crowne, the good-natured and true friend of Lenina, has the same second name since there are only ten thousand names available for the two billion inhabitants in the World State. She is representative of the girls who behave strictly according to their conditioning. That is why she admonishes Lenina not to have sex only with Henry Foster for too long a time. Though like Lenina she is not inclined to be promiscuous sometimes, she feels obliged to have sex with several men at the same time because "one's got to

play the game. After all, everyone belongs to everyone else" (p. 43). As she does not feel well, she follows her physician's advice to have a Pregnancy Substitute rather early at the age of 19, which causes the illusion of being pregnant. Though she is not as pretty and "pneumatic" as Lenina she admires her without being envious. When she sees that Lenina is sad because John does not make advances to her, she advises her friend to take soma to become courageous and take the initiative to seduce the Savage.
Though Lenina Crowne deviates from an orthodox behaviour when she seems to be faithful to Henry Foster, likes the outsider Bernard and desires the Savage more than anybody else, she is conditioned to be used as a sexual playmate and is therefore unable to understand John's love.

Helmholtz Watson

The Alpha-Plus Helmholtz Watson, who is Bernard's friend though he does not like his self-pity and boasting, is a lecturer at the Writing Department of the College of Emotional Engineering and also works as an Emotional Engineer in the Bureau of Propaganda where he writes propaganda texts and hypnopaedic slogans. His superiors believe that he is "a little too able" (p. 63), which foreshadows his being sent to the Falklands later on. Whereas Bernard is physically defective, i.e. too small, Helmholtz is characterized as strong and handsome. But because of his "mental excess" he is dissatisfied with his work and success in sport, with women and with his communal activities. Instead of writing propaganda texts he longs for writing something important though he does not know what it might be. Because of their "defects" the two friends feel that they do not really belong to the community of the brave new world. They know that as individuals they are different from the people who are conditioned to be happy with their life and work. But contrary to Bernard, who is shunned by others because of his "ugliness", Helmholtz deliberately decides to be alone.
Helmholtz, who is Bernard's true friend, confides to Bernard that he would like to write something different from propaganda, something that is really meaningful since he feels that he has "got something important to say and the power to say it" (p. 65). But as he does not know what to write about, he asks himself: "Can you say something about nothing?" (p. 66) After he has written his poem about Solitude he thinks that he is "just beginning to have something to write about" and feels really happy because he is able to use the "latent power" inside him. When he meets the Savage they immediately become friends since they both like Shakespeare's works though Helmholtz considers Shakespeare a perfect propagandist and is not able to understand Juliet's grief because of his conditioning.
Contrary to Bernard, he is courageous and, being a faithful friend, he defends the Savage against the attacks of Delta workers.

In his talk to the Controller when Helmholtz again expresses his wish to write something important and finds it "idiotic" to write when there is nothing to say, Mustapha Mond praises the "enormous ingenuity" required to create "works of art out of practically nothing, but pure sensation" (p. 192). But obviously Helmholtz had already begun to write something relevant when he gave his poem about Solitude to his students. As it is directed against a fundamental hypnopaedic lesson, he has come into conflict with Authority and is finally sent to the Falklands by the Controller who personally likes Helmholtz' spirit though he must disapprove of it officially. When he allows Helmholtz to go to the island of his choice, Helmholtz decides to go to the Falkland Islands because he believes that the rough climate there is favourable for writing.
To sum up, Helmholtz is a character who tries hard to discover his creativity and become a writer who has to say something despite the limits of his conditioning. Possibly he will break his chains since according to the Director "Alphas are so conditioned that they do not have to be infantile in their emotional behaviour" though "it is their duty to be infantile, even against their inclination" (p. 88) as long as they live in the brave new world. But as Helmholtz leaves the restrictions of the brave new world and is going to meet "the most interesting set of men and women to be found anywhere in the world", he has the opportunity to develop his own ideas. He is going to live together with "all the people who, for one reason or another, have got too self-consciously individual to fit into community-life" and are dissatisfied with orthodoxy and have got "independent ideas of their own" (pp. 196 f). They might also stimulate Helmholtz' writing.

John the Savage

The very first time the Savage appears, he is described as a young man with blonde hair, blue eyes and a white though sun-burnt skin who speaks Shakespearean English. He envies the bloodstained victim of the Indian ceremony and uses quotations from Shakespeare's *Macbeth* to express his feelings. When he sees Lenina, he seems to fall in love with her at first sight as if they were Romeo and Juliet. He is the son of the Director and his girl Linda, who got lost on the Reservation, where John was born and has grown up between the two cultures of the Indians and his mother's hypnopaedic education. He likes his mother's lullabies though he cannot grasp the meaning of the words. His mother taught him to read but he is unable to understand her book about practical instructions for Beta workers.
As he is neither fully accepted by the Indians nor able to understand his mother's promiscuous behaviour and conditioning, he is an outsider and feels deserted and lonely on the Reservation though Linda seems to love him as far as she is able to despite her conditioning. In his loneliness he discovers

"Time and Death and God" (p. 119). He is told the Indians' story about the creation of the world and taught Indian craft by an old Indian. When he gets an old edition of Shakespeare's works, he becomes capable of expressing his emotions and passions and tries to understand everything with the help of Shakespeare's words. In trying to kill his mother's lover Popé he identifies with Hamlet, and when he is looking forward to going to the brave new world where such a pretty girl as Lenina lives (cf. p. 122), he quotes Miranda's words.
But when he is supposed to admire the technological and economic progress in the brave new world, he expresses his disappointment by referring to Ariel in Shakespeare's *The Tempest* (cf. p. 138) or begins to vomit after having seen the Delta-Minus and Epsilon Semi-Moron workers in a factory. At Eton College Bernard is not able to answer his question about what the Alpha-Plus pupils are learning. The students are unable to understand the life on the Reservation and are prevented from reading literature such as Shakespeare's works since there are only reference books in the school library. John is also horrified by the stupid sex film he watches with Lenina; he leaves her though she expects to have sex with him, reads *Othello* instead and refuses to meet the important guests Bernard has invited to his party. When Bernard tells him that he is shunned by everybody and feels unhappy again, John replies: "I'd rather be unhappy than have the sort of false, lying happiness you were having here" (p. 156).
John identifies with Romeo and treats Lenina as if she were Juliet. He adores her, confesses his love and wants to marry her. But Lenina is unable to understand him because of her conditioning. When she wants to have sex with him, the Savage is terrified and pushes her away because he recognizes that she is a whore. He can neither establish a true love relationship between Lenina and himself nor a really strong mutual emotional relationship with his mother and himself because their conditioning and his Shakespearean view of reality are incompatible. Though his mother seems to recognize him before she dies, she also lives in a soma world of false dreams whereas John longs for her love, is overcome with grief and feels remorse. When he is horrified by the death-conditioning of children, he becomes aware of the brave new world as a nightmare (cf. p. 183). Moreover, his friendship with Bernard and Helmholtz fails because Bernard betrays him and Helmholtz is not really able to understand the deep and strong emotions expressed by Shakespeare. Despite his efforts of being a loving son and a true friend the Savage is totally lonely in the end.
In his discussion with the Controller John rejects comfort and a pleasant superficial life but insists on believing in God, freedom, the goodness of human nature and poetry. He claims the right to be a sinner, suffer pain and get old and sick. Contrary to the pseudo-happiness of the dystopian people, he also claims the right to be unhappy (cf. pp. 207 f).

When Helmholtz asks him why he looks sick and pale, he replies that civilization poisoned him. As the Controller does not allow him to accompany his friends Bernard and Helmholtz to the island because Mond wants to continue his experiment with him, he decides to retreat to a hermitage, an abandoned air-lighthouse in Surrey. But when he starts a new life there and whips himself to purify himself like an Indian, he is persecuted by the reporters of the sensational press and the sensation-seeking masses. When Lenina wants to see him he calls her a whore and frantically whips her. But finally he takes part in an orgy, wakes up desperate and full of remorse and commits suicide.
John the Savage is the protagonist in the second half of the novel. It is his main function to expose the brave new world as a nightmare, which causes his death.

Linda

Linda is a beautiful Beta-Minus working in the Fertilizing Room. She becomes pregnant accidentally when she has sex with the Director with whom she visits the Reservation but is left behind when she gets unconscious after falling into a crevice. She is rescued by the Indians and does not return to the brave new world since she feels ashamed of having a baby. She has to live outside the pueblo where she is treated like a whore and becomes a drunkard. As she is conditioned to consider childbirth and family life obscene, she raises her son John according to the hypnopaedic slogans and neglects and hates him sometimes but also loves him (cf. pp. 111 f). She behaves promiscuously and is despised and beaten by the wives of her sex partners. Her sexual relationship with the Indian Popé and her addiction to Indian drugs are shocking to her son who nevertheless loves her and tries to defend her. But as there is no medical care that helps people to look young until the age of sixty, she gets fat and old though she is only about forty years old. Moreover, she looks ugly and dirty because she cannot buy new clothes or mend her old ones and she has to live in unhygienic conditions without hot water outside the pueblo.
Though Linda is not able to answer her child's questions about technology and chemistry in the brave new world since she is conditioned to fertilizing work only, she tries to teach him how to read. When she and her son leave the Reservation and meet the Director she is happy to see him again. But as she looks old the inhabitants of the brave new world find her disgusting. Though she takes increasing doses of soma and is living in the dream world of the drug, she rarely recognizes her son. John who loves her very much visits her frequently in the brightly coloured Hospital for the Dying where she can watch TV and listen to synthetic music all the time and is stared at by the children who are being death-conditioned. Shortly before she dies at the

early age of forty-four, she recognizes her son, dreams of her Indian lover Popé and finally suffers the terror of death.
Linda is a split character between her conditioning as a Beta-Minus and her love to her son. She is neither able to live a decent life on the Reservation nor is she tolerated in the brave new world because of her old and unpleasant appearance. She dies as a tragic victim of the new world by getting and taking lethal doses of the drug that is supposed to make the inhabitants happy and contribute to social stability.

The minor characters

In the brave new world most of the inhabitants are industrially produced and conditioned as lower-caste workers without a name. They appear in groups of identical Deltas and Epsilons who are pleased with their work, entertainment and the daily ration of soma with the exception of an Epsilon-Minus-Semi-Moron, i.e. one of the lowest beings, who works as a liftman and joyfully awakes from his stupor when he sees the sunlight (cf. p. 56).
Henry Foster, the most competent fertilizer and predestinator in the London Hatchery and Conditioning Centre, and his friend, the Assistant Director of Predestination, are one-dimensional types who represent the totally conditioned conformists in the brave new world. They are only interested in sex, the consumption of sport and feelies and other superficial entertainments. Foster is Lenina's rather long-term sex partner, whereas she dislikes Benito Hoover, a "notoriously good-humoured" man who is said to be able to live without soma and whose invitation to go to the North Pole for a vacation Lenina rejects.
The Chief Justice and the Arch-Community-Songster of Canterbury, who is the highest religious representative in the brave new world, are used by Huxley to stress Lenina's promiscuity and the perversion of the dystopian society. The Arch-Community-Songster whose rank reminds of the former Archbishop of Canterbury rewards Lenina for having sex with him with a golden T, which has replaced the Christian cross since Ford is adored instead of God.
Some women such as Morgana Rothschild, Clara Deterding and others contribute to Bernard's inability to experience the mystic appearance of the Greater Being during the Solidarity Service.
Figures such as the Director of Slough Crematorium or Dr Gaffney, the Provost of Eton College, and others represent the goals of their institutions. Dr Gaffney who shows the Savage around is unable to understand the film about the Reservation but finds the Indians' flaggellation funny. Miss Keate, the Head Mistress at Eton, who is inclined to have sex with Bernard and disappointedly leaves him when the Savage stays away from Bernard's party, underlines the superficiality of the relationships in the brave new world.

The physicians Dr Wells and Dr Shaw treat their patients according to what they understand by health in the new world. Fanny Crowne for instance is made feel pregnant and Linda is given overdoses of soma and considered an interesting "example of senility in a human being" (p. 136).
Primo Mellon, a reporter of the upper-caste paper *The Hourly Radio*, and Darwin Bonaparte, who produces the feely *The Savage of Surrey*, arouse the curiosity of the inhabitants of the brave new world who stream to John's air-lighthouse in large numbers.
In comparison with the rather numerous characters in the brave new world, only a few Indians living on the Reservation are described, for instance Linda's degenerate sex partner Popé, whom John tries to kill out of hatred and who discovers Shakespeare's works in a chest, which are used by John to understand human emotions.
Mitsima, an old Indian at Malpais, teaches John all about Indian customs and craft. Other old Indians tell him stories about the Indian religion. When Kothlu and Kiakimé, whom John loves, marry, the Savage despairs and feels lonely. Palowhtiwa is envied by John because he is chosen as a victim in a cruel religious ceremony. But all the other Indians without a name are only mentioned to describe their religious ceremonies, their old age, their primitive and squalid living conditions, their sexual relationship to Linda and the revenge of their wives.
The Warden of the Reservation who has to control the visitors and prevent anybody from escaping talkatively describes the Reservation and thus conveys a general impression of the area to the readers.

Brave New World: A Dystopian Novel

Huxley's *Brave New World* belongs to the literary genre of the dystopian novel. Contrary to the Utopian novels that are written to convey the impression of a better world, dystopian novels are warnings of approaching a dehumanized future. Huxley, however, also uses terms such as fable and phantasy for his novel and Utopia and nightmare of the future for the brave new world described in it (cf. "Foreword", pp. 225, 233).

The first time the word Utopia was used by an author was in 1516 when the English humanist Sir Thomas More published his book *Utopia*, in which he describes an ideal future community of sensible human beings who tolerate all religions, guarantee education for all and have no private property. Before this, similar more or less "ideal" communities are described as the Garden of Eden in the Old Testament (Genesis 2–3) and in Plato's *Republic*, a state with a stratified society of philosophers, warriors and workers. This totalitarian state is ruled by philosophers who demand the sharing of goods, the equality of the sexes, the censorship of arts and the use of slaves. They also practise eugenics and do not allow unhealthy children to survive. Some of these motifs are also employed by Huxley who alters them according to his dystopian society such as biochemical birth control, the stratification of society and the Controller's cynical philosophy. Saint Augustine believes man to be a sinner throughout his life and as man totally depends on God's grace he can only become immortal in the mystical *City of God*, which is the title of his Utopia. In all these Utopias man is not really free but either ruled by a superior group of people or dependent on a supreme being, which is – in a perverted way – also characteristic of Huxley's dystopia where the inhabitants of the brave new world are controlled by a totalitarian ruler and conditioned to believe in Ford.

The Utopian novels written in the 18th and 19th centuries reflect the contrast between nature and the dangers of society and industrialization. In 1762, the French philosopher Jean-Jacques Rousseau published his educational Utopian book *Émile*, in which he describes the "noble savage" who once lived in harmony with nature whereas the present society is corrupted by civilization, which might also have inspired Huxley to a certain extent. Whereas the American Edward Bellamy believes in a better future and describes in his Utopian novel *Looking Backward* (1888) a socialist society where people are well-off and only work for honour, Samuel Butler and William Morris are sceptical about technological progress. That is why the people in Butler's *Erewhon* (1872), an anagram of "nowhere", have destroyed all machines since they endanger their work. Morris criticizes the uniformity of mass production and suggests the return to a pre-industrial society in his Utopian novel *News from Nowhere* (1891). In *A Modern Utopia* (1905) and *Men Like Gods* (1923), Herbert George Wells, who believed in scientific progress, describes a world state where everything is controlled but where man is able to improve and develop a noble mind, which Huxley did not believe when he began to write *Brave New World* as a satire on Wells' works. But he changed his mind during the writing process and considered his dystopia a warning of the misuse of science.

Against the backdrop of the two World Wars and the totalitarian Communist and Nazi regimes, dystopian novels reflect the suppression of human values. In his dystopian novel *We* (1925), the Russian writer Yevgeny Zamyatin describes the failure of the protagonist's resistance against the totalitarian regime of a Benefactor. Also Winston Smith, the hero in George Orwell's novel *1984* (written in 1948), unsuccessfully opposes the totalitarian state, where people are continuously observed by Big Brother and tortured and executed if they deviate from the rigid regulations, where science, art and literature are perverted and all historical records permanently falsified. Standard English has been replaced by Newspeak, the official language, which even prevents people from having "unorthodox" thoughts.

In his dystopian novel *Fahrenheit 451* (1954), Ray Bradbury describes a totalitarian society in which books are burned. The knowledge of history and reading old books is also considered dangerous in Huxley's brave new world. But Huxley describes a society where people are not suppressed by force as in Orwell's *1984* but kept under control by their biochemical production and conditioning since he wants to warn of the misuse of science. In his Utopian novel *Island* (1962), however, Huxley describes an "ideal state", which apart from several topics treated in *Brave New World* reflects his experiences with drugs and Eastern mysticism.

Utopian or dystopian novels that were recently written deal with more or less topical themes such as ecology and women's subjugation. Whereas in his *Ecotopia* Ernest Callenbach describes a newly founded Utopian state in western America which is based on ecological principles and dominated by women, Margaret Atwood's *The Handmaid's Tale* (1985) is a dystopian novel about the subjugation of women by the upper class in a totalitarian theocratic state founded after the overthrow of the government of the United States.

The genre of Utopian or dystopian novels has a rather long history. They either reflect the dreams of a better world or the nightmares of man's suppression and the loss of human values. Several motifs are dealt with by different writers such as the role of literature for education or – in a totalitarian state – its danger for the suppressors of humanity. Huxley for instance stresses the importance of Shakespeare's works for his protagonist to maintain human values in a corrupt society.

The Setting

According to the title of the novel, its setting seems to be more important than a differentiated description of the characters since they mainly represent the problems and themes Huxley is interested in and can hardly be classified as round characters. Even the Controller, Bernard, Helmholtz and Lenina predominantly play their roles in the brave new world and do not really change. This also applies to Bernard and Helmholtz because "Alphas are so conditioned that they do not have to be infantile in their emotional behaviour", but "it is their duty to be infantile, even against their inclination" (p. 88). If they do not adapt to the rules, they are banished to an island, which is the "punishment" provided for nonconformists in the brave new world. The Savage, however, is a more complex character since he represents the outsider both on the Reservation and in the brave new world. He is not accepted as equal by the Indians and feels isolated and lonely on the Reservation, and as he is not willing or able to adapt to the dystopian society he despairs and kills himself.

Referring to time the novel is set in the far future. It opens in the Central London Hatchery and Conditioning Centre in A.F. 632 (after Henry Ford's birth), i.e. in AD 2495 and presents a future world based on the principles of "Community, Identity and Stability". The dystopian World State was founded after the Nine Years' War, which began in A.F. 14 when the cultural heritage was destroyed, democracy abolished and the knowledge of history considered useless. Since the inhabitants of the World State are industrially produced and their total number is limited to two billion people they do not suffer poverty and can easily be supplied with everything they are conditioned to consume. As they live without strong passions, sickness, unemployment, war, the fear of death, etc but are conditioned to enjoy promiscuity, pseudo-religious services, sports and other kinds of entertainment, pain and trouble seem to have been eliminated. The people of the brave new world can take soma whenever they feel miserable. Nonconformists need not fear to be executed because they are only banished to an island, and also the Indians are not able to threaten the new World State because after being bombed their Reservation is fenced in and guarded.

The main geographical setting of the novel is the dystopian brave new world, which is the Western part of the World State with London as its capital. It is ruled by one of the ten World Controllers called Mustapha Mond who is the only Controller Huxley describes. The author does not inform the reader about the other nine states. The second important place in the novel is the Indian Reservation in New Mexico where the Savage grows up until he leaves it for the brave new world together with his mother Linda. Iceland and the Falkland Islands are only mentioned as places where the nonconformist

Alphas Helmholtz and Bernard will meet other interesting individuals after their banishment.
Other parts or places of the world are only briefly mentioned in connection with single topics dealt with by the Director, Henry Foster, the Controller or Bernard and Lenina whereas the members of the lower castes obviously do not know them. The Director for instance informs the students about the "progressive" work in the Hatchery Centres of Singapore and Mombasa (cf. p. 12) and Henry Foster mentions an earthquake in Japan that caused wastages in the Decanting Room (cf. p. 14). The Nile, Africa and the Mississippi-Missouri are only mentioned by him as parts of sentences used when hypnopaedia was unsuccessfully applied for intellectual education (cf. p. 26), and Kurfurstendamm and the Eighth Arrondissement in Paris are mentioned as places that were bombed during the Nine Years' War.
In his talk to the students the Controller mentions the islands of Samoa, New Guinea and the Trobriands to allude to natural birth or superstition. When he offers Helmholtz to choose an island where he will be sent to, he also mentions the Marquesas (cf. p. 198). He tells the Savage, Helmholtz and Bernard that the experiment of an Alpha society on Cyprus (cf. p. 193) and the experiment in Ireland to reduce the lower-caste working hours (cf. p. 194) failed. China is only mentioned to underline that science has been used in the brave new world to establish the most stable society in history, whereas China is "hopelessly insecure by comparison" (p. 197).
To underline the speed of the intercontinental rockets used for transportation, New York and Bombay are mentioned (cf. pp. 58, 138). Lenina remembers that she went to New York for a cheap weekend and to the North Pole for a holiday (cf. p. 80), and together with Bernard she flies over New Orleans, Texas and Santa Fé in order to travel to Malpais on the Reservation.
All these places and, additionally, several towns and seaside resorts in Italy, Britain and France are not meant to convey a coherent picture of the World State but they show that the geographical knowledge of the upper castes is not limited to the Western World. Apart from Bernard's and Lenina's flight over the Channel to Amsterdam, Bernard's wish to go for a walk in the Lake District and Helmholtz' idea to fly to Biarritz in his free time, mainly Central London, some of its suburbs and the surroundings of the capital of the brave new world are the setting for Huxley's novel. The former British government sector Whitehall for instance is now the Controller's Office, the former railroad station Charing Cross has become Charing-T Rocket Station, former Westminster Abbey has been transformed into the nightclub of Westminster Abbey Cabaret whereas St Paul's Cathedral was destroyed in the Nine Years' War. Big Ben and its chime have been replaced by a singing Big Henry.
Bloomsbury is the site of the former British Museum. Suburbs such as Shepard's Bush, Notting Hill, Ealing and towns around London like Stoke Poges, Torquay and Oxford have become sport centres, Chelsea an Abortion

Centre, Slough the central Crematorium. Exmoor, the high moorland in Southwest England, is used for picnics though the inhabitants of the brave new world are conditioned to ignore forests and beautiful landscapes. The Savage, however, loves nature and gardening when he retreats to his hermitage in Surrey. When Huxley describes John's route to the old air-lighthouse between Puttenham and Elstead, he mentions several places, among them his native town Godalming (cf. p. 209; see also the map in this study aid on p. 6).
London, its surroundings and some other places in England are described as void of former culture. Religion, ethics and the love of nature have been perverted according to the demands of the brave new world for technology, consumption, pleasure, pseudo-religious ceremonies, recycling of the dead, etc.
Contrary to the hygienic, healthy, consumptive and mechanized brave new world, the Reservation in New Mexico is described as a wilderness and wildlife habitat where the Zuñi Indians live in pueblos and go hunting. As the climate is hot, there is an unpleasant smell because of the squalor of their houses and surroundings. The Indians are naturally born, get sick and old. They believe in their ancient Indian god and Jesus and cling to their traditional values such as monogamy and family life, native crafts, rites and ceremonies. As their territory is surrounded by a sixty thousand volt wire fence that is supplied with electricity from the Grand Canyon hydro-electric station, they have no chance to leave the Reservation, which is illustrated by the countless skeletons of animals there.
The many different places also reflect Huxley's interest in geography and travelling whereas he owes his knowledge of Indian reservations in New Mexico to his friend D.H. Lawrence and to reading books about them.

The Social Hierarchy of the World State

From 1925 to 1926 Huxley travelled via India, Burma, Malaysia, Indonesia and Japan to the USA. The rigid hereditary Hindu caste system has probably also inspired Huxley to divide the dystopian society in *Brave New World* into five castes. According to Hindu belief, every individual is born into one of the castes without being able to leave it as long as he lives, which also applies to the caste members in the novel since they are biochemically conditioned and socially predestined. The Epsilons resemble the pariahs in India who belong to the lowest caste or are even outsiders and despised by the other castes. Certainly Huxley also had the British class system in mind when he satirically describes the dystopian society as highly stratified according to birth and occupation.

The stratified society of five different castes is controlled by one of the ten World Controllers, whose name is Mustapha Mond, the Resident World Controller of Western Europe. As the World State is based on Henry Ford's ideas such as the invention of the assembly line for mass production and the prejudice that the knowledge of history is useless, the belief in Our Ford has replaced Christianity. The five castes differ from each other mentally, referring to their work, concerning their living conditions and their clothes since Alphas wear grey, Betas red, Gammas green, Deltas khaki and Epsilons black. All of them are hypnopaedically conditioned to become class-conscious at an early age in order to be content with their specific roles in the dystopian society. Beta children are for instance sleep-taught to dislike playing with Epsilon children because they are too stupid and wear "a beastly colour". At the same time they are hypnopaedically conditioned to believe that they are not as intelligent as Alphas, who work too hard (cf. pp. 28 f).

The Hierarchy and Social Structure of the World State

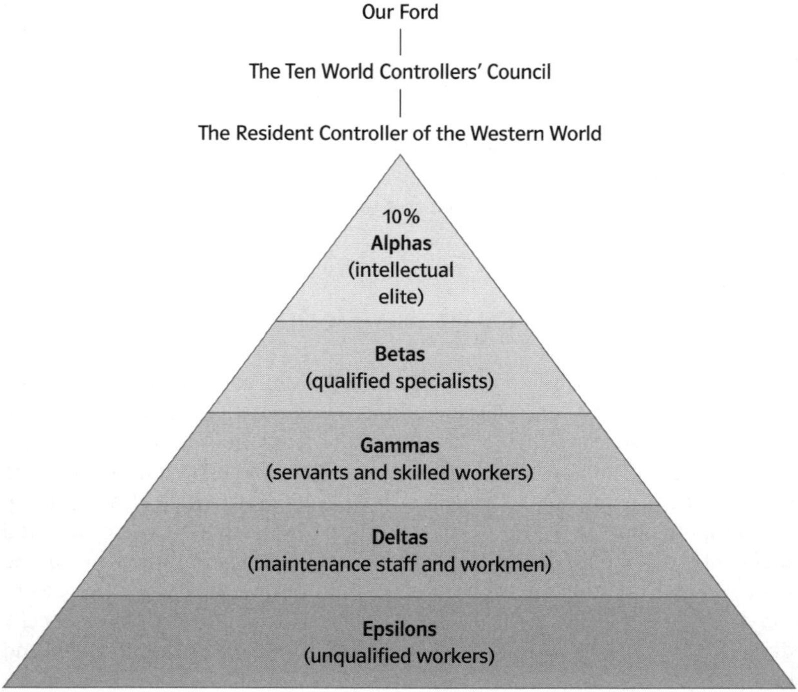

People in Huxley's dystopia never change but remain what they are predestined to be throughout their lives except Helmholtz, Bernard and the Savage.
The following sketch shows the hierarchy of the World State including the social stratification and the division of labour in the brave new world.
Only ten percent of the dystopian people are Alphas. Their caste is subdivided into the most intelligent Alphas-Double Plus, Alphas-Plus and ordinary Alphas. They are the elite in the brave new world and have the most important and demanding jobs or positions such as the Controller Mustapha Mond, the Director, the Chief Judge, The Arch-Community-Songster of Canterbury, Helmholtz Watson, Henry Foster, the Assistant Director of Predestination, Bernard Marx, the doctors Wells and Shaw, the Warden of the Reservation, the Provost of Eton and probably Miss Keaton, the Head Mistress at Eton College as the only Alpha woman in the novel. But she is not explicitly described as an Alpha, which also applies to the film producer Darwin Bonaparte and the reporter Primo Mellon. Thus the social hierarchy mirrors the predominance of males in the brave new world – and also in Huxley's time. Male Alphas are produced to hold all the powerful or important positions in the World State.
Alphas feel superior to the other castes with the exception of Bernard, who looks like a Gamma-Minus because of his faulty production. He feels rejected and despised by Alphas (cf. p. 36), is ridiculed and not considered attractive by Beta women and believes he is not respected as an Alpha by the lower castes (cf. pp. 61 f). Contrary to the other caste members, "Alphas are so conditioned that they do not have to be infantile in their emotional behaviour. But that is all the more reason for making a special effort to conform. It is their duty to be infantile, even against their inclination" (p. 88). The only characters who do not conform, Helmholtz Watson and Bernard Marx, are finally excluded from society and banished to an island.
The Alphas have sexual relationships to Beta females, who are qualified workers in the London Hatchery and Conditioning Centre. They are even only Beta-Minuses such as Lenina, her friend Fanny, Linda and probably the women who attend the Solidarity Service with Bernard. They have to be promiscuous and are considered more or less "pneumatic" by their Alpha sex partners. Whereas most of the women are produced as sterile "freemartins", Lenina, Fanny and Linda have to wear Malthusian belts to prevent pregnancy. Linda, however, gets pregnant by mistake and gives birth to John the Savage.
Since the Alphas and Betas feel superior to the lower castes of the Gammas, Deltas and Epsilons, Lenina for instance is happy that she is no Gamma or Epsilon (cf. pp. 60, 69) and looks down on them though she is hypnopaedically conditioned to know that all castes are needed in the brave new world: "Everyone works for everyone else. We can't do without anyone. Even Epsilons are useful. We couldn't do without Epsilons." (p. 68) Gammas are mainly servants, Deltas maintenance staff and Epsilons unqualified workers.

They are not allowed to fly in helicopters like the Alphas and Betas but have to use monorail trains and live in barracks. None of the members of the three lower castes is mentioned by name. Whereas Gammas and Deltas are also differentiated within their castes, e.g. into Gamma-Plus or Delta-Minus, Epsilons are called "Semi Morons". They are illiterates and for instance do sewage works (cf. pp. 17, 28). One of them, the Epsilon liftman, however, overcomes his robot-like stupor for a moment and enjoys the sunlight that makes "him start and blink his eyes" (p. 56).

The Main Ideas, Themes and Motifs

The dystopia of the brave new world reflects Huxley's central ideas, interests and his wide reading and knowledge of literature. Critics think that the novel is not really a narration with various round characters in a complex situation but mainly a novel of ideas. Huxley himself admits that he is not much interested in the characters' life and fate but in presenting his knowledge and favourite ideas and topics: "I'm not very good at creating people; I don't have a very wide repertory of characters. These are difficult things for me." (Huxley, "The Art of Fiction (1960)", interview; https://www.theparisreview.org/interviews/4698/aldous-huxley-the-art-of-fiction-no-24-aldous-huxley)

The misuse of science

At the very beginning the reader is immediately confronted with the misuse of science. Instead of protecting family life and natural birth, the people of the dystopia are industrially produced in bottles on assembly lines. The knowledge of biochemistry, genetic engineering and cloning enables the production of the required number of people who are differentiated into five castes according to their functions in society. The Delta and Epsilon embryos are even multiplied to become identical clones and are made nearly stupid by adding a high amount of alcohol to their blood surrogate, which causes brain damage. The population of the World State does not surpass two billion people.

Huxley stresses the absurdity of biological experiments even more when the Director of the London Hatchery and Conditioning Centre expresses his ambition to break the records of the Centres in Mombasa and Singapore where up to 17,000 identical adults from one ovary are produced. Eugenic experiments in Mombasa even prove that it is possible to produce identical beings that are both sexually mature and full-grown at an earlier age, which Huxley ridicules when the Director mentions that the production of such beings who are about six years old is socially useless since they are too stupid to replace even Epsilon workers (cf. pp. 12, 18).

Pavlov's psychological theory is misapplied when the infants are conditioned to hate books and nature and consume sex and sport instead. Freud's theory is misused to abolish family life in order to prevent psychological conflicts and neurotic passions. The Controller is so enthusiastic about Freud that he even exclaims "Our Freud" instead of "Our Ford" when he speaks about psychology (cf. p. 39). By intensive sleep-teaching the children are conditioned to behave promiscuously and be eager to consume new products according to the frequently repeated slogans. Even their language is manipulated since words referring to natural birth and family life such as mother and father are considered obscene, which means that everybody is supposed not to use them and eventually to forget what they mean. As little children are hypnopaedically conditioned to become promiscuous and play sex games at an early age, they learn that sex is only fun and has nothing to do with procreation or love. Women are considered "pneumatic" like a sofa or shoes and treated as "meat", which is both degrading and ridiculous.

In order to eliminate love, pain, misery and the fear of death people are conditioned to have no strong passions or deeper feelings. They are entertained by synthetic music and superficial films, enjoy various kinds of sport, and are content with the work they are programmed to do. They are called "happy" but in fact are deprived of all human feelings.

Though the inhabitants of the brave new world are said never to become sick, there are doctors in the dystopian state. But they misuse medicine. Though most of the women are produced as sterile "freemartins", some of them remain fertile because their ova are required for the continuous production of new embryos. As they are not allowed to become pregnant, they wear contraceptive Malthusian belts. If they do not feel well, they are prescribed a Pregnancy Substitute. Dr Wells even gives it to Fanny earlier than usual (cf. p. 38). If anybody needs to be passionate, he or she has to undergo a Violent Passion Surrogate treatment. Vaccination is not primarily meant to protect people against a serious disease such as sleeping sickness but to enable them to work in the tropics. Whenever anybody feels miserable and does not know how to cope with an unpleasant situation or just wishes to be high, he or she can take or is given soma, which is used as the normal or ultimate drug to guarantee the stability of the dystopian state. Dr Shaw is pleased to have the opportunity of studying an example of senility and allows Linda to take lethal overdoses of soma since she is of no use for the dystopian society. Moreover, he cynically argues that "soma may make you lose a few years in time" but gives you "the enormous, immeasurable durations [...] out of time. Every *soma*-holiday is a bit of what our ancestors used to call eternity." (p. 135)

Whereas before and during the Nine Years' War chemistry was used to invent explosives such as TNT and poisonous gas, 2000 pharmacologists and biochemists had to develop soma in A.F. 178, which they could industrially produce six years later. It is considered the perfect drug with a "euphoric,

narcotic, pleasantly hallucinant" effect and without any dangerous side-effects if taken in adequate doses (cf. pp. 51 f). The upper castes take it whenever they wish to and also decide themselves which dose is required to overcome difficulties or go on a "soma holiday". They are offered the drug by friends or in drinks and ice-cream at parties or during Solidarity Services in order to have the hallucination of Our Ford's appearance. Rations of the drug are distributed to the lower castes after work every day to keep them content. When the Savage tries to free Delta workers from their drug-addiction, he causes their revolt and is arrested by the police since he endangers social stability. Thus the whole dystopian society is fundamentally drug-addicted. The Controller defends the use of soma as harmless contrary to the drugs that were used in former times such as alcohol, morphine and cocaine (p. 51) and cynically states: "Christianity without tears – that's what soma is" (p. 205). The Indians, however, drink the alcoholic mescal and take the cactus drug peyotl that produces visions and makes people feel sick afterwards.
At the end of the novel the Controller explains why pure science is no longer allowed. At the same time he admits that he deceives himself: "I'm interested in truth, I like science. But truth's a menace, science is a public danger. As dangerous as it's been beneficent. It has given us the stablest equilibrium in history" (p. 197). The Controller, who had the choice between true science and power, decided to misuse science for political goals, i.e. for establishing a totalitarian state, to forbid the publishing of a new biological theory as dangerous and to restrict research and innovation since science is no longer necessary to find truth and enlarge people's knowledge. The ultimate goal of science is the production and conditioning of people who are happy with their specialized work, with consumption and entertainments.

Political and economic control and manipulation

Since liberty and democracy have been abolished after the Nine Years' War, people live in a totalitarian state ruled by a Controller who believes that it is his duty to make people "happy" though he regrets that he has given up science. The World State is run by the Controllers' Council which consists of ten Controllers. Mustapha Mond is responsible for the Western World with London as its capital. This "brave new world" is based on the principles Community, Identity and Stability. People are no longer born to be free individuals who have the right to pursue their individual happiness but are programmed to be always together with others. They are no real individuals but conditioned to behave according to their caste.
After the Nine Years' War and the great Economic Collapse, which allude to the First World War and the Great Depression from 1929 to 1934, the mass production and conditioning of people are meant to guarantee the political and economic stability of the World State. Whereas before destruction,

under-production and under-consumption undermined the political and economic order, the inhabitants of the brave new world live in peace and are "compelled to consume so much a year. In the interests of industry." (p. 48) Reading old books, studying history, pure science and art have been abolished since they distract people from work and endanger the stability of the dystopian world that is based on conditioning for specialized industrial and agricultural work, consumption and pleasure. That is why also the cultural heritage has been destroyed, for instance cathedrals such as St Paul's and other historical monuments, museums such as the British Museum and libraries of old books. The Controller states: "Our Ford Himself did a great deal to shift the emphasis from truth and beauty to comfort and happiness." (p. 197) As science was misused for the production of bombs, it has been restricted and is controlled in the World State. The purpose of science is no longer truth but the "happiness" of the people.
As Ford is the economic idol of the dystopian state, his ideas of mass production and consumption are considered essential means to produce both people and goods. The assembly line also requires the division of labour, specialization and shift work, which means full employment, cost saving and the incessant production of bulk goods people can afford such as in Ford's time the legendary Ford T-Model. Electric advertising is installed to attract people to the movies and night clubs.
As the inhabitants of the brave new world are conditioned only to consume new goods and never to mend or repair anything, they live in a throwaway society. The goal of consumption is to keep industry going and guarantee work. As the working hours of the lower castes could easily be reduced, an experiment in Ireland proved that the workers become dissatisfied and do not know what to do in their additional spare time. Consequently they go on working in shifts for longer hours than necessary.
The dystopian people are only conditioned to pleasure and distraction and never experience true happiness since they are deprived of the fundamental human rights. When Henry Watson sententiously says: "All men are physico-chemically equal" (p. 68), Huxley alludes to a perversion of the American Declaration of Independence (1776): "We hold these truths to be self-evident, that all men are created equal, that they are endowed by the Creator with certain unalienable Rights, that among these are Life, Liberty and the pursuit of Happiness." The people of the brave new world do not have the fundamental human rights such as equal opportunities irrespective of birth, status, sex, race, etc, or the right to have a family, freedom of speech and equal justice. Contrary to the Declaration of Independence, the World Controllers do not derive their power "from the consent of the governed". People do not have the right to abolish despotism and are unable to comprehend what true life, liberty, and the pusuit of happiness mean.

Dystopian technology

Before the Nine Years' War science and technology were for instance misused to produce gas bombs and other devastating explosives. In the dystopian state, however, science and technology are needed to produce people and provide them with modern conveniences. As Ford's invention of the assembly line made the mass production of cars possible and is now applied to biology and the industrial production of the dystopian people, technology is an essential element in the World State.

When Huxley first visited Los Angeles, Chicago and New York in 1926, he did not like the busy and crowded cities of fun and pleasure. That might be a reason why the dystopian Guildford near his native town Godalming only consists of seven skyscrapers (cf. p. 210) and the dystopian London is described as a city of high-rise buildings. The huge Hatchery and Conditioning Centre for instance contains 4000 rooms. The largest rooms are used for the industrialized production and manipulation of embryos on assembly lines. Moreover, there are conditioning rooms, dormitories for sleep-teaching, play rooms for 900 older children, etc. The changing rooms and bathrooms contain all technical conveniences such as vibro-vacuum massage machines, perfume tube automats and synthetic music machines. Men have an electrolytic shave which burns the hair off and use eau-de-Cologne taps. Different perfumes are used permanently and frequently change as long as the dystopian people live. The Savage even thinks that perfume is Lenina's "essential being" (p. 124). All these technical inventions also contribute to a comic effect of the novel.

In the brave new world, Lupton Tower at Eton College is fifty-two storeys high and the building of the Bureaux of Propaganda and the College of Emotional Engineering have sixty storeys. The Hospital for the Dying is a sixty-storey tower where the dying people can watch TV all day and night, listen to synthetic music and smell perfumes that are automatically changed every fifteen minutes.

The flat tops of the skyscrapers are used as airfields for the private-owned helicopters or rocket-planes and the roof of Charing-T Tower is a platform for intercontinental passenger rockets flying to New York or Bombay. Whereas the upper castes travel in such fast aircraft, the lower castes commute in monorail trains. Cars are only mentioned once when the police arrest the Savage and his friends.

The many large sports centres such as the Electro-magnetic Golf Course and the Escalator Fives Courts for tennis are technology parks. The names of the apparatus-based sports sound both "modern" and ridiculous, for instance Centrifugal Bumble-puppy, Riemann-surface tennis and Escalator Squash (cf. pp. 31, 59, 64).

The entertainments industry provides the population with TV sets, synthetic music boxes, scent and colour organs, etc. Electric advertising in huge letters

is meant to attract people to visit dancing and music halls but also makes the starry sky invisible. The reporter of *The Hourly Radio* who tries to interview the Savage at the end of the book directly broadcasts the words spoken into a microphone via antennae on his aluminium hat, which contains a wireless receiver and transmitter, to London where the paper is printed and sold in the streets only eight minutes later (cf. pp. 215 f).
There are agricultural factories and the crematorium is a factory for the production of phosphorus, which is needed as fertilizer. Henry Foster proudly states: "Fine to think we can go on being socially useful even after we're dead. Making plants grow" (p. 68). Natural things are frequently replaced by synthetic products such as blood surrogate, acetate and viscose clothes, fake marble, etc, and buttons are replaced by zips.
Contrary to the Indians' natural and uncivilized life on the Reservation, the dystopian people live in a highly mechanized and synthetic world. Speed and time-saving inventions are characteristic of the brave new world since technical comfort has replaced reflection and contemplation.

Sensational mass media

In the brave new world all the film producers, composers, reporters, college lecturers, writers, etc are propagandists or have to provide people with entertainment and sensational news to contribute to social stability (cf. pp. 62 f).
There are three London papers each for a different caste. The most demanding paper, *The Hourly Radio*, is published for Alpha readers. Gammas are only able to understand the less demanding *Gamma Gazette* and Deltas *The Delta Mirror* because it contains only words of one syllable. Epsilons are too stupid to read and write at all. Sensational news are directly transmitted by the reporter of the Alpha paper, which is printed and sold immediately.
TV and film producers and composers have the task to entertain people with stupid sex films and synthetic music. Films are called "feelies" because they cannot only be seen and heard but also felt, which first irritates the Savage and then makes him feel sick. Whereas the dystopian people inclusively Lenina enjoy the primitive sex scenes and sequences of adventurous actions, John finds the film base. Huxley's description of the Savage's reactions to the titillations he feels stresses the comic effect of the scene.
Helmholtz Watson is the most skilled Emotional Engineer and an excellent lecturer at the College of Emotional Engineering. He produces articles for *The Hourly Radio*, composes film scenarios and writes slogans and hypnopaedic rhymes. As he is a lecturer by profession he combines teaching with propaganda but is dissatisfied with his job.

The perversion of religion

Ford has become the idol of the dystopian society and replaces God since Christianity has been abolished after the Nine Years' War. Whereas the Indians worship their ancient god Pookong and Jesus, the inhabitants of the brave new world have to recognize Ford as the Supreme Being who is celebrated on Ford's Day, at Community Sings and Solidarity Services.
People must take part regularly in Solidarity Services, where they repeatedly sing long Solidarity Hymns after being welcomed by the President, who makes the sign of the T instead of the Christian cross. Instead of bread and wine Christians receive during the Holy Communion, the dystopian people are given soma tablets and drink from "the loving cup of strawberry ice-cream soma" (pp. 74f) in order to feel the coming of the Greater Being and experience their mystical unification with "Our Ford". They conjure him up by singing the second hymn and expressing their wish to die because "when we end, / Our larger life has but begun" (p. 75). In fact they are deluded into a state of ecstasy and are not able to realize the truth since they will be burnt in the Crematorium when they are dead and disappear as a cloud of gas. The Solidarity Service that resembles a big drug-party ends with ecstatic dancing until everybody takes part in an orgy of group sex.
There is no belief in eternal life after death. It is replaced by the hallucinations after taking soma. Dr Shaw states: "Every soma-holiday is a bit of what our ancestors used to call eternity" (p. 135). Mustapha Mond cynically explains why the brave new world is dependent on soma: "And if ever, by some unlucky chance, anything unpleasant should somehow happen, why, there's always soma to give you a holiday from facts. And there's always soma to calm your anger, to reconcile you to your enemies, to make you patient and long-suffering. [...] Anybody can be virtuous now. You can carry at least half your morality about in a bottle. Christianity without tears – that's what soma is" (p. 205). Thus soma is used to prevent people from perceiving and accepting reality and facts. They are not really virtuous since they are unable to decide autonomously what is good and what is bad.
As all inhabitants of the dystopia are conditioned to enjoy work and distractions, are never sick, do not fear pain and death, do not have any idea of sin, remorse or life after death and can take soma whenever they wish, their cycle of life is always the same independent from their caste and position in society.
All of them are industrially produced and conditioned to their caste-specific roles in society. They work and are entertained until they die at the age of sixty, dissolve into a cloud of gas and are replaced by a new embryo that is industrially developed and conditioned, etc.

Man's Cycle of Life in the Brave New World

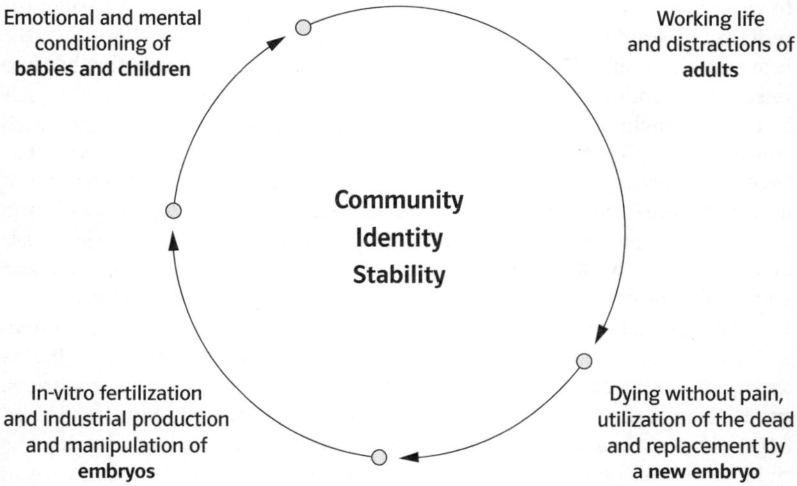

The reversal of values

Huxley's *Brave New World* was written with his pessimistic view of America's and Europe's cultural future in mind. When he visited America in 1926, he disliked the crowded cities and their entertainment industry. In his travelogue *Jesting Pilate* (1926) Huxley criticizes the American "revaluation of values". But his dystopian novel also mirrors his view of the British class society.

The dystopian people in *Brave New World* are deprived of all fundamental human rights. They are not born free but industrially produced and conditioned to identify with the goals of the totalitarian state and the caste they belong to. They are not able to pursue happiness because they are not able to know what it is since it has been replaced by fun, pleasure and distraction. Instead of personal love, marriage, family life, free education and free choice of career, people are sleep-taught to have promiscuous sex and to consider words such as birth, mother and father obscene. Every kind of behaviour that deviates from the dystopian norms is called "abnormal" or "unorthodox" such as the little boy's wish not to take part in sex games (cf. p. 32) or Bernard's wish to be alone or discover his individual self. The "orthodox" dystopians, however, are never alone. Since they are conditioned to feel "happy" only as a part of the community, they are even afraid of loneliness and would not know what to do if they were on their own. Thus

they also do not learn anything about history, literature and art which are considered useless and dangerous. As every caste member is conditioned to like his or her specific work, a change of professions and careers is impossible. In the brave new world everybody has lost his individuality and freedom is replaced by conditioning and "predestination".
Scientists are no longer supposed to enlarge human knowledge but are misused to produce and manipulate people. Science is restricted to the goals of the dystopian state and to a large extent replaced by technology which contributes to comfort and convenience. The former Christian Service has become a Fordian drug party ending with group sex. The mass media do not inform people about political, economic and cultural events but entertain and distract them by sensational news and sex films. The dystopian people are neither able to think creatively nor to have strong passions, feel sorrow and pain or fear death. They are kept continuously "high" by taking soma.
The only character in the novel that is not conditioned and therefore able to think and feel like a real human being is the Savage. He rejects a life in dystopian comfort and pleasure but wants poetry, danger, freedom, goodness, sin. He claims the right to go hungry, to feel pain, to worry about the future, to get sick, to grow old, ugly and impotent. In short, he insists on having the right to be unhappy (cf. pp. 207 f). Thus Huxley underlines that contrary to the dystopian people who are condemned to be "happy", human beings are given the opportunity to choose and to experience real life which is both joyful and sad. Whereas the conditioned people in the brave new world are deprived of human morality and responsibility, the Savage has the chance to decide and act as a moral being.

The lack of education

Already at the beginning of the novel the reader is confronted with the topic of education. The Director describes the industrial biochemical production and conditioning of man and partly explains its relevance for the World State to the male students who uncritically write down every word: "Straight from the horse's mouth into the note-book. The boys scribbled like mad." (p. 8) They do not think themselves but automatically accept what they are told. As they have been hypnopaedically conditioned according to the principles of the dystopian society, they are neither able nor expected to put real questions. Instead they take everything for granted the Director and the Controller say: "The students nodded, emphatically agreeing with a statement which upwards of sixty-two thousand repetitions in the dark had made them accept, not merely as true, but as axiomatic, self-evident, utterly indisputable" (p. 40). Thus they are not considered unique individuals who should be helped to critically expand and advance their knowledge on their own and develop their spiritual, social and ethical values.

As there are no families in the brave new world, children do not have the opportunity of learning anything from their parents, grandparents or other members of the family. There is no pre-school education since in the so-called Infant Nurseries the toddlers are shock-conditioned to hate books and nature all their lives (cf. p. 23). Reading books is considered a waste of time for the lower castes and the higher castes might be reconditioned when they read the "wrong" books. As the children even fear to look at flowers or touch and smell them, their sense organs are conditioned for the rest of their lives. Moreover, the dystopians are only given the possibility to listen to synthetic music and will never be able to appreciate any other kind of music.
Instead of loving nature, the inhabitants of the brave new world have to love country sports because then they must use transport and consume manufactured goods. Contrary to Bernard, Lenina for example likes to take part in Obstacle Golf and watch the Women's Heavyweight Wrestling Championship, ignores nature but is terribly frightened by the night, the moon, unruly weather, etc (cf. pp. 81 f), whereas the Savage enjoys nature and gardening (cf. pp. 211 ff).
Sleep-teaching is used to manipulate the children's minds totally by the "suggestions from the State". The hypnopaedic slogans are permanently repeated "till at last the child's mind is these suggestions, and the suggestions is the child's mind. And not the child's mind only. The adult's mind too – all his life long" (p. 29). Moreover, the children play erotic games to become promiscuous and games which afford apparatus to increase consumption. In order to make them fearless of dying, they are death-conditioned when they visit the Hospital for the Dying. They do not understand what death is and do not respect the dying but are noisy and play the erotic game hunt-the-zipper. At first they stare at Linda "with the frightened and stupid curiosity of animals" (p. 177), but when she is dead they are grinning and eating chocolate éclairs (cf. pp. 181 ff).
Whereas Epsilons are not able to read and write because their brains were intentionally damaged by the Fertilizers, and do not attend school at all, Alpha boys and girls exclusively visit Eton College where they are prepared for their work in the biochemical industry and for sex life. The super intelligent Alpha-Double-Plus pupils also learn elementary relativity, which Bernard is not able to explain to the Savage. When pupils in the geography room are shown a documentary film about the Reservation they are – due to their conditioning – not able to take the pictures of the Indians' remorse seriously but find them ridiculous. In the school library there are only reference books that inform them about what they are allowed to learn in dystopia. Instead of reading literature, for example Shakespeare's works, the pupils are supposed to go to the feelies if they want to be entertained. Literature, which is disqualified as mere entertainment, is considered dangerous in the brave new world because it could destabilize society.

To sum up, children are conditioned and manipulated to fit in the dystopian society without being able to live an alternative life. They are withheld every information that could "recondition" them. They are not educated to become open-minded, creative and critical adults and free and responsible individuals but are manipulated to be what the dystopian state wants them to be according to the principles Community, Identity, Stability.

The Author's Point of View

The narrator of the dystopian novel tells the story from an omniscient third-person point of view. He is able to describe the outer and inner action since he knows what the characters are doing, thinking and feeling. He describes the mass production and conditioning of the different caste members by telling how the Director of the Hatchery and Conditioning Centre informs a group of students. The narrator gives further background information about the World State through the Controller who informs the students about its principles and history and in detail explains his position and goals to Helmholtz, Bernard and the Savage.
The narrator seems to be objective and detached even when the different characters express their emotions and feelings, their thoughts and criticism. But according to Huxley he adopts the role of a satirist who implicitly or explicitly ridicules or criticizes the abuse of human values.

Form and Structure of the Novel

The novel consists of 18 chapters, each of a different length. The novel can be subdivided into seven parts:

Chapters I–III:	Description and reasons of the production and conditioning of people
Chapters IV–V:	Relationships between Henry Foster, Lenina, Bernard and Helmholtz
Chapters VI–IX:	John's and his mother's life on the Reservation
Chapters X–XIII:	John's disgust of the brave new world and its lack of love
Chapters XIV–XV:	John's mother's death, his revolt and arrest together with Bernard and Helmholtz
Chapters XVI–XVII:	Their discussion with the Controller and Bernard's and Helmholtz' banishment
Chapter XVIII:	John's retreat and suicide

John's revolt in Chapter Fifteen is the turning point and climax of the action of the novel because he is arrested together with his friends Helmholtz and Bernard who are banished to an island.
If the novel is not so much considered a novel of action but of ideas, its climax is reached in Chapter Seventeen when during his discussion with John the Controller runs out of arguments. Concerning John's isolation, remorse and suicide the novel has a tragic ending.

Forms of Discourse, Language and Style

As *Brave New World* is a dystopian novel, Huxley employs the main stylistic device of this literary genre: He presents a negative Utopian world in a satirical way by making use of exaggeration, irony, parody and ridicule in order to criticize the abuse of human values. Moreover, he uses various poetic and rhetorical devices to stress the different characters' words and behaviour to challenge the reader to analyze the absurdity of the World State and its reversal of values. Though the novel can predominantly be considered a novel of ideas, the plot and the main characters are presented in a rather eventful and varied way to heighten the reader's interest and arouse his or her response.

Forms of discourse: narration, description, argument and persuasion

Since the novel is a narrative fictional text, Huxley tells his story about the future in the past. He presents a series of events and describes how the characters behave and what they think and feel by frequently using dialogues and direct speech. Thus Huxley describes the setting of the first chapter, the building of the London Hatchery and Conditioning Centre, at the beginning of the novel and introduces the Director as the first character of the book by his lecture to the students: "'And this,' said the Director opening the door, 'is the Fertilizing Room.' […] 'I shall begin at the beginning'" (pp. 8 ff). Huxley also makes use of telling a story within a story when the Savage describes his growing up on the Reservation (Chapter Eight), or the author uses a telephone call without telling what the caller says (cf. pp. 172 f). The reader, however, can easily derive everything from the words of the receiver of the call.
As Huxley presents several main characters such as Bernard and Helmholtz, who to a certain extent deviate from the totally conditioned caste members and do not fully adapt to the dystopian society, and the Savage, who is the main critic of the dehumanized World State, the author employs the form of

discussion to convey the characters' controversial ideas. The discussion between Helmholtz, Bernard, the Savage and the Controller in Chapter Sixteen, which mainly consists of the Controller's explanation and justification of the World State, seems to be predominantly a **persuasive text**. But it also conveys background information and thus enables both the characters and the reader to understand the cynicism behind the dystopian world. The discussion between John and Mustapha Mond in Chapter Seventeen, however, in which the Controller is not able to refute the Savage's arguments, can be understood as an **argumentative text**. This also applies to the Savage's speech which he delivers in front of a mass of Delta workers to convince them that soma is "poison to soul as well as body" (p. 184) without recognizing that they are not able to understand his reasons against the drug.
Huxley's dystopian novel reflects his wide knowledge of literature and language, in particular Shakespeare's works, which is not surprising since he studied English literature in Oxford.

Varieties and levels of language

Huxley predominantly uses Standard English but sometimes also informal language and several other varieties of English and technical terms.

Scientific terms

To arouse the reader's interest the novel begins with the use of pseudo-scientific terms and the fundamental dystopian slogan in incomplete sentences the reader does not yet comprehend. By the description of the totally sterilized fertilizing room and the industrial production of embryos an unpleasant atmosphere is created, which causes the reader to become suspicious.
As many of the technical terms are commonly known such as laboratory and microscope, Huxley uses them to underline the misuse of sciences, in particular biology, chemistry, biochemistry, pharmacology, medicine and psychology, for the industrialized production and conditioning of the dystopian people, e.g. ovum, spermatozoa, incubator, embryo, vaccination, syringe, blood transfusion, oxygen, X-rays. Apart from soma, the so-called perfect drug invented by the author, drugs such as alcohol, morphia, cocaine, mescal and peyotl are mentioned to stress their hallucinatory or fatal effects. Other medical terms such as peritoneum ("Bauchfell"), diaphragm ("Zwerchfell"), thyroxin ("Schilddrüsenhormon"), lupus, corpus luteum, endocrine, pituitary, ophthalmia etc allude to Huxley's interest in medicine and his wish to study medicine, which he could not realize because of his eye-sickness. Moreover, he mentions illnesses such as anaemia, typhoid and sleeping sickness. The enumeration of dystopian

medicaments, however, underlines the absurdity of medical treatment in the brave new world (cf. p. 39).
Some of the chemical elements or compounds Huxley mentions are certainly known to the reader, e.g. lead, chlorine, magnesium, calcium carbonate and caustic soda ("Ätznatron"). But when the Controller refers to the First World War and enumerates several poisonous gases such as phosgene, chloropicrin and hydrocyanic or when chemical formula for instance of the explosive TNT and phosphorus pentoxide are mentioned by the author, the average reader can only understand them when he uses a glossary or consults a special dictionary, which is also necessary to understand several medical terms. But it is not necessary to look up all of them to understand the novel. Huxley also likes to invent terms that cannot be found in a dictionary such as placentin (extract from the placenta).
Some terms are used in a different sense such as Hatchery, Fertilizer (original meaning: substance to make plants grow better) and decant (originally: to pour wine from one container into another). Terms such as Bottle-Liner, Matriculator, Predestinator and Decanting Room are used to describe the different stages of the production process. Moreover, Huxley uses several fictitious names and words such as Bokanovsky's Process and its derivations bokanovskyfy, bokanovskification and Podsnap's Technique whereas the Neo-Pavlovian Conditioning Rooms allude to Ivan Pavlov's experiments with dogs. Various other terms that are misused refer to different disciplines such as Kant's categorical imperative and Freud's psychoanalyst terms trauma and fixation. When the Director is still haunted by fantasies, dreams and thoughts about the loss of Linda, Huxley refers to Freud's psychoanalytic theory (cf. p. 87 f).
Words and terms taken from the fields of physics and technology are meant to stress dystopian progress such as selenium cell, elementary relativity, helicopter-planes, monorail trains and intercontinental rockets for passengers. Huxley also coins new words for helicopters used as taxis or sports planes such as taxicopter and sporticopter (cf. pp. 149, 185). Musical terms such as tattoo, blues, A flat major and many well-known Italian terms such as tremolo, alto, tenor, falsetto, capriccio, diminuendo are used ironically to describe the synthetic music in the brave new world. In order to describe the different sounds of the synthetic music machine, Huxley changes the names of traditional instruments, e.g. hyper-violin, super-cello and oboe-surrogate (cf. p. 146) and sexophone. The words "feely" (p. 147) and "flivver" (p. 185) are also Huxley's neologisms. As he was interested in movies and later became a film script writer in Hollywood, he also uses film terms such as close-up, slow motion, sound track (p. 218).
Huxley's use of scientific and special terms reflects his wide reading knowledge in many fields of science and underlines that his dystopian novel is mainly written for educated people though it is frequently not necessary to

fully understand the meaning of the terms since most of them merely illustrate their misuse in the dystopian society.

Varieties of English, levels of language and foreign languages

Though most of the text is written in a language used by adults, Huxley sometimes also employs "baby talk" or extra verbal communication and children's speech to show certain levels of pre-language development and childlike behaviour in some of his characters. Thus the babies in the Neo-Pavlovian Conditioning Rooms crawl towards the display of beautiful children's books and roses while giving "little squeals of excitement, gurgles and twitterings of pleasure" (p. 22). "Pussy and cock-a-doodle-doo and baa-baa black sheep"are words known from English nursery rhymes (cf. p. 23). When a lorry driver sees that the Savage is whipping himself, he exclaims "Ford!" whereas his twins use the pet name "Fordey!" (p. 213). Linda uses the pet name Tomakin instead of Thomas, when she meets the Director again, which underlines her emotional relationship to him and in that situation has a comic effect on the reader.
Colloquialisms such as "Hoity-toity" (p. 52) are sometimes used. Spoken English is rather frequent, for instance in the dialogues of Bernard and Lenina. They use simple words, everyday language, short and one word sentences, abbreviated sentences, questions, repetitions, exclamations. The dialogues of Mond, Helmholtz, Bernard and the Savage, however, reflect the knowledge of educated people. Whereas the explanations of the Director that he gives to the students is rather a conceited lecture of an expert, the speeches of the Savage and the Voice (cf. pp. 184 ff., 187) that are addressed to Delta workers are mainly argumentative or persuasive.
Sometimes Huxley makes use of extra verbal communication to convey the impression of spoken language, for instance "Eh?", or to ridicule the stupidity of the "feely" and the audience: "Oo-oh, Aah" (p. 183).
Old-fashioned or informal words, for instance "bunk" in Ford's narrow-minded statement "History is bunk" (p. 35) or "smut" to degrade true science and old books (cf. pp. 25, 202), are sometimes used to refer to the past or to stress the lack of reflection in the brave new world. Swear words and offensive words are used by Bernard to insult a person, for instance "Ass!" (p. 17), or express dissatisfaction or disgust, e.g. "I damned well wish ..." (p. 83), "Idiots, swine!" (p. 53), "Damned whore!" (p. 170). Huxley does not use taboo words but when he describes the reversal of values he mentions that words such as birth, father and mother are considered obscene by the inhabitants of the dystopian society. Bernard does not even dare to write the complete word of mother in his report to the Controller (cf. p. 140).
Pseudo-religious terms and speech is employed to satirize the misuse of Christian terms and to describe the revaluation of values, e.g. President instead of priest, the sign of the T, the loving cup of strawberry ice-cream soma, the

incarnation of the Greater Being, His Coming, Solidarity Hymn, supernatural Voice, procession of dancers, the liturgical refrain Orgy-porgy, the ecstasy of the community (cf. pp. 74 ff.) and the perverted use of the words blasphemy (cf. p. 78) and sacrilege (cf. p. 186). Religious terms are also used to describe the Indian rites and ceremonies and the Savage's desperate praying to the Christian God and the Indian god Pookong and his self-torment to purify himself from his sins (cf. pp. 210 f).

Huxley uses a lot of words taken from different fields, e.g. various names of animals, plants and landscapes when he refers to the children's conditioning (e.g. rose, primrose, nightingales, cuckoo, bees), the Reservation (for instance lizard, porcupine, turkey buzzard, puma, corn) or John's hermitage in Surrey, Huxley's home county, e.g. lark, gorse ("Stechginster"), juniper ("Wacholder"), rushes ("Binsen"), heath, fir. As the brave new world is described as civilized and hygienic, perfumes or sweet scents such as eau-de-Cologne, thyme, lavender, patchouli, verbena, etc are spread nearly everywhere, e.g. in the dressing rooms, in the dancing hall by the scent organ or in the Hospital for the Dying to convey a pleasant atmosphere. Lenina, however, is disgusted by the natural smells on the Reservation.

Though French, German and Polish are called dead languages (cf. p. 25) and Spanish and the Indian languages such as Zuñi and Athapascan are extinct languages (cf. p. 92), some Spanish and French words are used, e.g. "Penitentes" (p. 142) and "petits beurres" (p. 219), even Latin words: "corpus luteum" (p. 15). When Huxley describes the Indian Reservation he uses Spanish words such as mesa, pueblo, tortilla, canyon and the Indian ceremony chamber kiva and mentions the Zuñi turquoise jewelry, moccasins, totemism, corn song and dance and ancestor worship (cf. pp. 97, 113, 115). The Zuñi language used by Mitsima and the Savage is at least partly invented by Huxley (cf. p. 115). It is used by John to express his unwillingness to meet dystopian people. But as several Zuñi words are repeated in similar situations and accompanied by words such as "Go to hell!" or "menacingly", the reader can understand what the Savage wants to express (cf. pp. 151 f, 220).

Style

Huxley's style is to a large extent ironic since his purpose is to warn and ridicule. Moreover, he makes use of various poetic and rhetorical devices.

Satire, irony, sarcasm, humour and jokes

Brave New World can be read as a satire since the novel describes the dystopian society in an ironical way, ridicules it by exaggeration and implicitly or explicitly criticizes its absurdity.

Huxley ironically uses the word "wisdom" in connection with hypnopaedia (cf. pp. 42, 82), which is only practised in the brave new world to make

children and adults like Lenina unable to think critically. This is also underlined by the stupid laughter of the students, the Eton "elite", Helmholtz and the dystopian people about serious human and literary topics (cf. pp. 27, 132, 141, 161, 225).
Ford's statement "History is bunk" is not only a prejudice but an expression of total ignorance since the reader is aware of the importance of historical knowledge for the present and future life and perhaps even for the survival of the human being. It is also evident that education is impossible without true scientific research and unlimited reading, which also the Controller is fully aware of. Freedom and happiness cannot be achieved by producing people without a unique individuality and by conditioning them to mistake sex for love, pleasure for happiness, conditioning for education and conformity for responsibility.
Several times Huxley uses perverted sayings such as "What man has joined, nature is powerless to put asunder" (p. 23) or "Ford helps those who help themselves" (p. 178). Moreover, he sometimes replaces irony by sarcasm, e.g. when the Controller refutes John's belief in God as natural for human beings: "'You might as well ask if it's natural to do up one's trousers with zippers,' says the Controller sarcastically." (p. 202)
Huxley tends to describe people and situations in a comic way, for instance by the use of hyperbole: "Helmholtz had had 640 different girls in four years" (p. 64). When Bernard for instance tries to concentrate on the Solidarity Service, he is irritated by Morgana Rothschild's enormous black eyebrows that meet above the nose (cf. p. 71) and the ridiculous ecstasy of the women when they feel the Greater Being's coming. The description of the Savage's feelings and sensations while watching the stupid sex feely "Three Weeks in a Helicopter" is a comic parody on similar films (cf. pp. 146 f). Huxley also uses or changes names in a comic way, e.g. Big Henry (instead of Big Ben), the Singery clock: "Big Henry sounded the hour. 'Ford', sang out an immense bass voice from all the golden trumpets. 'Ford, Ford, Ford …' Nine times." (p. 73)
Comic effects are also achieved by Huxley's choice of words and several neologisms. Thus he describes the dystopian police as "goggle-eyed and swine-snouted in their gas-masks" (p. 186) and he coins neologisms like zippicamiknicks and zippijamas when he mentions Lenina's clothes with zips (pp. 125 f). It is also ridiculous to call women such as Lenina and Fanny "pneumatic" or "too pneumatic" sex partners since the word is also applied to sofas and shoes (cf. pp. 57, 74, 65, 214). Sometimes Huxley plays with words, e.g. when he changes "saxophones" to "sexophones" and compares their sound to the mewing of cats: "The sexophones wailed like melodious cats under the moon" (p. 70). Even Ford is believed to sit in a "flivver", which is only a small, cheap and old car, possibly the mass-produced Ford T-Model (cf. pp. 43, 75). Also extra-verbal exclamations for instance in the feely or

produced by the spectators have a comic effect. The same applies to the many onomatopoetic sounds such as “zip” and “dab”.
Apart from the many hypnopaedic slogans also various dialogues, names, rhymes, quotations and comparisons have a comic effect though they seem to be used seriously by the characters of the novel or even by the author.
All these stylistic devices are used to ridicule and criticize the dystopian society. Huxley mostly criticizes the perverted dystopian society implicitly by describing the characters' conditioned thoughts and behaviour. But sometimes his criticism is explicit, for instance when he mentions the stupid laughter of the dystopian Alpha children, pupils and adults about family life and human values. Huxley expresses his criticism and warnings in particular through the Savage with whom he seems to identify to a large extent, since John struggles to maintain the fundamental human values, also based on his knowledge of Shakespeare's works. Thus Huxley enables the reader also to enjoy reading the novel though his topic is serious and his main purpose is to criticize and to warn the reader of a similar future.

Names

The names Huxley gives to the dystopian institutions, sports and articles sound more or less ironical or ridiculous, e.g. the Hatchery and Conditioning Centre since the word hatchery normally refers to a place for hatching eggs of birds or fish. Whereas the game “Centrifugal Bumble-puppy” (p. 31) refers to a children's game with a ball attached to a post by a string and thus makes sense, “Riemann-surface tennis” (p. 59) sounds ridiculous since the German mathematician Georg Riemann uses the word surface with many planes to represent complicated mathematical functions. The reader is also hardly able to imagine how to play Escalator Squash or Electromagnetic Golf (cf. pp. 53, 64). Also Big Ben with its worldwide appreciated chime is ridiculed as Big Henry, the Singery clock (cf. p. 72).
Sometimes Huxley invents names such as Bokanovsky and Reuben Rabinovitch but due to his wide reading knowledge he likes to use the names of famous historical figures for his characters. Some of the names refer to famous writers, musicians, scientists, psychologists and politicians, for instance Shaw, H.G. Wells, Pfitzner, Helmholtz, Marx and Engels, Darwin, Pavlov, (Napoleon) Bonaparte, who are well-known to educated readers though not to the dystopian people since the knowledge of history and the use of historical books is prohibited in the brave new world. In most cases the characters, for instance the two doctors, do not have anything in common with their famous namesakes. This also applies to Polly Trotsky, a little girl playing sex games (p. 27), and the women taking part in the ridiculous Solidarity Service: Morgana Rothschild (name of a banker family), Fifi Bradlaugh (British social reformer), Joanna Diesel (inventor of the diesel engine), Sarojini Engels (co-author of the Communist Manifesto). Frequently the first and the second

name of the characters contradict each other and thus have a comic effect on the reader, e.g. Polly and Trotsky or Fifi and Bradlaugh. Benito Hoover is described as a character who is always good-humoured, but neither his first name that seems to refer to the Italian fascist dictator Benito Mussolini nor his second name that possibly alludes to the 31st President of the United States or to the vacuum-cleaner mirror his character. Some other names Huxley uses refer to the historical figures such as the Indian chief Palowhtiwa and Popé, a medicine man who revolted against the Spanish oppressors, though the character in the novel is his disgusting caricature.
The Controller's name Mustapha Mond seems to refer to Alfred Mond, the founder of ICI, one of the largest British chemical industries and to Mustafa Kemal, called Kemal Atatürk, the chief founder of modern Turkey as a secular or to a certain extent "westernized" state. Possibly Huxley establishes a relationship between Atatürk's goal of modernizing Turkey and the Controller's position of the Resident Controller of the Western World.
But the first name of Darwin Bonaparte, "the Feely Corporation's most expert big-game photographer" (p. 217), who shoots a film about the Savage as if John were a gorilla seems to allude to the misunderstanding of Darwin's theory of evolution. After seeing the film the masses want to see the Savage and throw – "as to an ape" – peanuts and other "food", which again ridicules the misinterpretation of Darwin's theory whereas the allusion to Napoleon might underline the film producer's power over the masses.
Huxley even strengthens the comic effect when he applies men's names such as Engels to women or derives the first name of Lenina from the Russian revolutionary. Possibly he also wants to allude to the dubiousness of the Communist Revolution. When he calls one of the doctors Dr Wells, it is perhaps a sideswipe at his famous contemporary author of science fiction and utopian novels since Huxley's original intention was to write a satire of Well's utopian novel *Men Like Gods* (1923) when he began to write *Brave New World*.
Several names, however, allude to Huxley's central fields of interest though the characters themselves do not represent them, e.g. Helmholtz Watson. His first name reminds of the German physiologist, physician, physicist and mathematician who investigated sight and sound, which Huxley was certainly interested in because of his eye-sickness. Watson refers probably to John B. Watson, an American behaviourist who studied the relationship between stimulus and response, which is also related to Pavlov's experiments with dogs and the Neo-Pavlovian Conditioning Rooms in the novel.
Some names, for instance Malthus and Freud, are frequently used by Huxley since like Malthus he was also worried about the problem of overpopulation. Birth control is dealt with when the fertile women in the novel have to wear Malthusian belts, take part in Malthusian drills and dance Malthusian Blues (cf. pp. 49, 71, 72) to be always aware of preventing pregnancy since the total population of the World State is not allowed to surpass the limit of two

billion people. "Our Freud" seems nearly as important for the dystopian society as "Our Ford" because Freud's theory is misused to justify the abolishment of family life and Freud's psychoanalysis is reflected in several motifs of the novel such as Mustapha Mond's criticism of the family and the Director's bad dreams due to his guilty conscience.

Ford's invention of the assembly line and mass production is the prerequisite for the continuous industrial production of the dystopian people. His devaluation of history as "bunk" is adopted to justify the dystopian people's ignorance of the past.

Mustapha Mond does not only mention Henry Ford's biography but also some titles of religious books, e.g. written by the Catholic theologian Cardinal Newman or the French statesman and philosopher Maine de Biran, who was interested in mysticism like Huxley (cf. pp. 189, 199 ff).

Some names allude to Huxley's biography. When he was at Eton, there was a school clerk called Gaffney like the Provost in the novel. The name of Miss Keate alludes to the very strict former headmaster Dr John Keate, which might have amused readers who also attended Eton College in Huxley's time. Because of his love of classical music Huxley also mentions Mozart and excellent singers (cf. p. 146) to ridicule the synthetic music in the brave new world.

Though the characters in his novel are generally not characterized by their names and Huxley seems to make fun of the famous historical figures, he also warns the reader that not only in the dystopian future society, where only 2000 names are available for all people, the achievements of the famous scientists, biologists, psychologists, etc might be misused or forgotten. There would also be the danger of ignoring or playing down the fatal consequences of the deeds and ideologies of Napoleon, Lenin, Mussolini and in particular the anarchist Bakunin, who intended to replace social stability by chaos.

Propaganda and poetry

Helmholtz Watson is described as one of the best writers of slogans and hypnopaedic rhymes at the Propaganda House and as a lecturer at the College of Emotional Engineering. Thus many of the hypnopaedic slogans which are permanently repeated throughout the novel were written by him. Every slogan expresses one of the fundamental aspects of the brave new world its inhabitants are conditioned to take as self-evident. The slogans are applied in sleep-teaching for "moral education, which ought never, in any circumstances, to be rational" (p. 27) or "moral propaganda" (p. 157). Since hypnopaedia is "words without reason" (p. 29) there is no difference between education and propaganda. The hypnopaedic slogans are "Suggestions from the State" (p. 30) and reflect the central motto of the World State, "Community, Identity, Stability". The goal of hypnopaedic conditioning is that "the sum of the suggestions is the child's mind. And not the child's mind only. The adult's mind too – all his life long." (p. 29)

The slogan "Everyone works for everyone else. We can't do without anyone. Even Epsilons are useful" (p. 68) suggests that though there are different castes, they all are one community and contribute to the stability of the dystopian society, which is even strengthened by the production of identical groups of Delta and Epsilon workers.
Despite the slogan that everybody is useful for society the children are conditioned to become class-conscious, i.e. proud of belonging to the caste they were produced for. Thus they are conditioned to be prejudiced against the other classes, because Beta children are sleep-taught to believe that they are better and cleverer than Gammas and Deltas: "Oh no, I don't want to play with Delta children. And Epsilons are still worse. They're too stupid to be able to read and write. Besides, they wear black, which is such a beastly colour. I'm *so* glad I'm a Beta." (p. 28) Delta children, however, are conditioned to be content with their work and do not wish to be Alphas since Alpha children "work much harder than we do" (ibid.). There is no upward mobility in the brave new world and no risk to lose one's higher position since everybody is conditioned to remain what he or she is as long as they live.
Since the state's stability is also based on permanent production and consumption, the dystopian people are conditioned to have a throwaway mentality: "But old clothes are beastly"; "We always throw away old clothes. Ending is better than mending" (p. 48); "The more stitches, the less riches" (p. 107).
As love is replaced by sex, the dystopians are suggested to behave promiscuously by the permanent repetition of the hypnopaedic slogan "Everyone belongs to everyone else" (p. 40). If anything goes wrong, there is always soma to restore stability, suggested by the permanent repetition of the hypnopaedic slogans and rhymes: "A gramme is better than a damn" (p. 52) and "A gramme in time saves nine" (p. 82). The people are made believe that "Everybody is happy nowadays" (pp. 69, 83) and are suggested to follow the hypnopaedic slogan "Never put off till tomorrow the fun you can have today" (p. 85). The technical comfort of vibro-vac, synthetic music, etc and the dystopian sports facilities contribute to health and the feeling of wellness supported by the slogan "Progress is lovely" (p. 90). "Civilization is sterilization" (p. 98) or the childish rhyme "Streptocock-Gee to Banbury T, to see a fine bathroom and W.C." (p. 107) strengthen the hypnopaedic suggestion to love hygiene and live without infections.
Huxley makes use of several parodies of songs that mirror aspects of the dystopian society and the people's conditioning. When Lenina is in a good mood because she is looking forward to watching a feely with the Savage, she sings a trivial "love" song, in which love is compared to soma: "Hug me till you drug me, honey" (p. 145). In the Westminster Abbey Cabaret a favourite song is played whose text praises the Bottle instead of a lover with the refrain "There ain't no Bottle in all the world / Like that dear little Bottle of mine"

(pp. 70 f). This parody of a love song containing the non-standard form of "ain't" and double negation seems to ridicule similar simple songs in the roaring twenties. Nowadays the word 'bottle' could be easily replaced by the word 'baby' in modern pop songs.
In order to strengthen the sense of community, there are "Ford's Day celebrations and other massed Community Sings" (p. 73). Bernard takes part in a Solidarity Service where the community has to sing three long solidarity hymns that conjure up the appearance of Ford and are supposed to send the singers into ecstasies supported by taking soma. When the service finally turns into an orgy they sing "Orgy-porgy, Ford and Fun" (p. 78), the corrupted version of the nursery rhyme "Georgy Porgy".
When John is a baby, Linda sings lullabies which refer to the brave new world and hypnopaedic slogans such as "Streptocock-Gee to Banbury T" and "Bye, Bye Banting, soon you'll need decanting" (p. 109). Thus Huxley changed the well-known English nursery rhymes "Ride a cock horse to Banbury Cross" and "Bye, Baby Bunting, Father's gone a-hunting". When Linda is dying, the Savage remembers "the childish rhymes" such as "A, B, C, vitamin D: The fat's in the liver, the cod's in the sea" as "magically strange and mysterious" (p. 176) since they remind him of their life together on the Reservation and his mother's care and – to a certain extent – love. Huxley also employs rhymes that were once used in England to teach children to read when Linda teaches her son: "The Cat is on the Mat. The Tot is in the Pot" (p. 113).
Helmholtz Watson who longs to become a real poet writes a poem about loneliness, which is a "blasphemy" in the brave new world and thus causes his banishment to the Falkland Islands. The poem which consists of two stanzas each with twelve lines deals with silence and empty streets at midnight and asks how to fill this emptiness better than now (cf. p. 158).
Whereas the slogans, rhymes and songs mirror the conditioning of the dystopian people, Linda's lullabies and childlike sentences express a deeper feeling for her son than she is conditioned to. They underline that children love rhymes even if they do not fully understand them. Helmholtz Watson's poem proves that he begins to "say something" that is more valuable than propaganda and hypnopaedic rhymes.

Quotations from Shakespeare's works

As Huxley studied English literature in Oxford, he has a wide knowledge of Shakespeare's works. In *Brave New World* he refers to fifteen Shakespearean tragedies and comedies and to the poem *The Phoenix and the Turtle* but only to one history play, *King John*. He could assume that at least the English educated readers would understand the quotations and the allusions to several Shakespearean works. According to the Savage's inner conflicts, Huxley most frequently refers to *Hamlet*, *Romeo and Juliet*, *Troilus and Cressida*, *Othello*, *King Lear* and *Macbeth* and, of course, to *The Tempest*.

Already the title of the novel *Brave New World* refers to Shakespeare's play *The Tempest* (V,1,181–184), where Miranda, who has grown up on an island with her banished father, exclaims when for the first time she sees the arrivals from Italy:

> […] O, wonder!
> How many goodly creatures are there here!
> How beauteous mankind is! O brave new world,
> That has such people in't!

As apart from her father there is only the savage Caliban on that island, Miranda admires the beauty of the visitors like John in Huxley's novel when he admires Lenina's beauty and is looking forward to accompany Bernard and Lenina to the brave new world where he expects to meet more likeable people. But Huxley employs the quotation in an ironical way, which he underlines by Bernard's question: "And, anyhow, hadn't you better wait till you actually see the new world?" (p. 122) Huxley seems to have borrowed the motifs of the Savage and the islands from Shakespeare's play and changed them according to his conception of the traditional noble Savage.
When the Savage is looking forward to leave the Reservation he expresses his joy by repeating the exclamation "O brave new world" three times (pp. 120 f) though he is totally ignorant of Lenina's conditioning and the dystopian society. But when he observes the work process in a factory and the robot-like low-caste workers and repeats Miranda's words twice "by some malice of his memory", he finally runs out of the factory to vomit (cf. p. 140). After his mother's death he is horrified when he sees the masses of identical Delta workers waiting for their soma rations. He uses Miranda's words now five times in a sarcastic way (cf. pp. 183 f) and feels urged to stop the distribution of the drug since Miranda who "was proclaiming the possibility of loveliness, the possibility of transforming even the nightmare into something fine and noble. 'O brave new world!' It was a challenge, a command." (p. 183) But again Shakespeare's words prevent the Savage from recognizing that his attempt at changing the dystopian people's minds is illusionary.
As the Savage uses Shakespeare's works, which he got on the Reservation by Popé at the age of twelve, to understand everything better and express strong emotions, he is not able to make a difference between literature and reality but runs the risk to misunderstand people's thoughts, wishes and behaviour. On the other hand, Shakespeare's works enable him to recognize immorality and the violation of human values.
The first time the Savage uses Shakespeare's words in the novel is after the cruel Indian ceremony (cf. p. 103) when he points to the bloodstains on the floor and asks Bernard and Lenina "in a voice that trembled with emotion": "Do you see that damned spot?" But Huxley's use of Shakespeare's "damned spot" taken from *Macbeth* (V,1,30) is ironical since the Savage would have

liked to be accepted as worthy to be the sacrifice in the religious ceremony and would have given such a lot of blood that "the multitudinous seas [would] incarnadine" (*Macbeth* II,2,65). The words "damned spot", however, are used by Lady Macbeth when she is haunted by the King's murder and tries to wash the imagined blood from her hands before she finally commits suicide. The second quotation refers to Macbeth's horror after the King's murder, whereas the Savage expresses his deeply felt disappointment. Thus the Savage misapplies Shakespeare's words the very first time he uses them, which he also does several times later. On the other hand, the Savage's reference to *The Merchant of Venice* (II,1,1) when the dark-skinned Prince of Morocco says: "Mislike me not for my complexion", corresponds to John's statement "They disliked me for my complexion" because with his white skin and blonde hair he looks different from the Indians.

As the Savage is disgusted at his mother's and Popé's sexual relationship, he identifies with Hamlet, who is urged by his father's ghost to avenge his death because he was murdered by his brother, who married Hamlet's mother only two months after the murder. Hamlet's words intensify the Savage's hatred: "Nay, but to live / In the rank sweat of an enseamed bed, / Stew'd in corruption, honeying and making love / Over the nasty sty" (III,4,91–94) though his attempt at killing Popé fails (cf. pp. 113 ff).

After having fallen in love with Lenina at first sight (cf. p. 104), the Savage frequently quotes from Shakespeare's plays such as *Troilus and Cressida* (I,1,54 ff; III,2,162 f), *Romeo and Juliet* (III,3,36 ff; I,5) and *The Tempest* (IV,1,15 ff) (cf. pp. 125 f; p. 168) to express his admiration of her beauty and his love or to stress her innocence and virginity (as he believes) in contrast to his shyness and unworthiness. He identifies with Ferdinand in *The Tempest* who praises Miranda as "perfect" and "Of every creature's best" (III,1,47 f) by replacing Miranda's name with Lenina's (cf. III,1,37; p. 166). Moreover, the Savage "was seeing himself as Romeo and Lenina as Juliet" (p. 160). But Huxley makes use of irony again since the Savage praises Lenina like a saint though she is conditioned to be promiscuous. When he realizes this, he calls her a whore and refers to corresponding lines in *The Tempest* (IV,1,25 ff), *Timon of Athens* (IV,3,116 f), *King Lear* (IV,6,112 f; 122 ff), *Othello* (IV,2,67 f; 71 ff; 81), etc (cf. pp. 168 ff). Finally, he whips Lenina by repeating the Shakespearean word for prostitute "strumpet" several times (pp. 217, 222).

The Savage also mixes up "soma-holiday" and "eternity" (p. 135) when he thinks of Shakespeare's play *Antony and Cleopatra* (I,3,35). He ridicules the speed of the intercontinental passenger rockets because they are slow in comparison with the airy spirit Ariel (cf. p. 137) in *The Tempest*. When he sees the caskets of soma (p. 144), he is – ironically – reminded of Portia's three caskets of gold, silver and lead in *The Merchant of Venice* (II,7,2 ff).

The Savage and Helmholtz Watson become friends through poetry. But Helmholtz is only able to appreciate the – in his view – "propaganda"-like

language of Shakespeare's poem *The Phoenix and the Turtle* and is totally unable to understand Romeo's and Juliet's deeply felt emotions of love and grief (cf. pp. 160 ff). The Savage continues to refer to Shakespeare's plays, for instance to *Othello* to express his disgust of the feely but the Controller, who admits that *Othello* is better than the feelies (cf. pp. 190 f), explains why Shakespeare's works cannot be understood in the brave new world: "Because our world is not the same as Othello's world. You can't make flivvers without steel – and you can't make tragedies without social instability" (p. 191). True art has been sacrificed to stability, comfort, well-being and entertainment, which the Savage rejects as "told by an idiot" (*Macbeth* V,5,26).
In his talk to the Controller, the Savage tries to understand the religious writings mentioned by the Controller by referring to his experience of loneliness and to Shakespeare's *King John*, *Hamlet*, *King Lear* and *Othello*. He recites Edgar's words from *King Lear*: "The gods are just, and of our pleasant vices / Make instruments to plague us" which Edmund confirms and states that "The wheel is come full circle [...] (V,3,171–176; pp. 207 f), which the Savage understands as "God managing things, punishing, rewarding" (p. 203). He believes in God but cannot find any words in Shakespeare's works to explain God (cf. p. 199).
When the Savage broods over death at the end of the novel, Huxley quotes several well-known lines from *Macbeth*, *Hamlet* (II,2,184; III,1,64), *King Lear* and *Measure for Measure* (III,1,17 ff), for instance:

> And all our yesterdays have lighted fools
> The way to dusty death.
> (*Macbeth* V,5,21 f)

> As flies to wanton boys, are we to the gods
> They kill us for their sport.
> (*King Lear* IV,1,36 f)

The references to Shakespeare, who frequently compares death and sleep in his plays, represent antithetical and also contradictory views of death and the influence of higher powers on man's life without giving a final answer.

Literary, cinematic and rhetorical devices
Huxley employs several literary and rhetorical devices rather frequently to underline his view of the brave new world. Some parts of the novel are written in a way that reminds of a film script or shooting script.
He makes frequent use of antithesis, contrast and paradox for example to describe and stress the difference between the brave new world and the Reservation. Whereas the dystopian people live a sterile, healthy and "happy" life in peace and comfort, the Indians live in squalor, become sick, suffer pain and live in primitive circumstances. Ford and the dystopian celebrations are contrasted with Indian gods and Jesus and with the traditional Indian

ceremonies. Contrary to conditioning and manipulation of the dystopian castes, the Indian people live in families though they are not really free because their Reservation is a large prison without any possibility to escape. The five castes in the brave new world differ from each other concerning the colour of their clothes, their physique, mental abilities, work, means of transportation, etc.

The most important antithesis Huxley uses is the discrepancy between the Savage's view of life and the Controller's cynical principles. Their confrontation at the end of the novel mirrors the many contrasting aspects of total control and freedom such as promiscuity vs. love, pleasure vs. happiness, misuse of science vs. true science, pseudo-religious manipulation vs. personal belief, solitude and community: "it is natural to believe in God when you're alone" vs. "But people are never alone now [...]. We make them hate solitude; and we arrange their lives so that it's impossible for them ever to have it" (p. 203). That is why Huxley frequently introduces sentences with "but" or employs antonyms such as horrible vs. lovely (cf. p. 149) and forms antithetical sentences to underline opposite ideas such as slavery and freedom, e.g.: "Linda had been a slave, Linda had died; others should live in freedom, and the world be made beautiful." (p. 183)

Huxley confronts the dystopian way of life with Shakespearean values, for instance impersonal relationship and promiscuity with individual beauty and love, which is for instance expressed in the Bottle song (cf. p. 71) in a stereotype language in contrast to Romeo's poetic words of admiration and use of images (p. 155):

> Bottle of mine, it's you I've always wanted!
> Bottle of mine, why was I ever decanted?
>   Skies are blue inside you,
>   The weather's always fine;
> For
> There ain't no Bottle in all the world
> Like that dear little Bottle of mine.

> "O, she doth teach the torches to burn bright!
> It seems she hangs upon the cheek of night
> Like a rich jewel in an Ethiop's ear;
> Beauty too rich for use, for earth's too dear."
> (*Romeo and Juliet* I,5,48–51)

Sometimes Huxley makes use of paradox, e.g. when Bernard calls Helmholtz his "victim-friend" (p. 157) or Mustapha Mond cynically states: "But as I make the laws here, I can also break them." (p. 190)

Huxley frequently uses stylistic devices that contribute to a graphic and ironical style such as comparison and metaphor, for instance when Lenia is compared to meat (cf. pp. 51, 84) and Helmholtz calls Bernard a rhinoceros (cf. p. 80).

The comparison of the increasing sounds of a helicopter to insects from hornet over wasp to mosquito and the decreasing noise from wasp, hornet, bumble-bee, cockchafer to finally stag-beetle (cf. pp. 52 ff) is both graphic and ironic. At the end of the novel he compares the “swarm of helicopters” to locusts and metaphorically describes the helicopters as grass-hoppers (cf. pp. 219 f).
Metaphors are also used when the flat top of mountains is “the great mesa ship” with a “gunwale” or a “deck of stone” (p. 97). The Controller calls the dystopian people “nice tame animals” (p. 190). Metaphorical language is for instance used when Bernard’s and Lenina’s way to Malpais is described as the “steep path zigzagged” (p. 97) or the Savage says: “I ate civilization” (p. 208).
One of the most important stylistic devices is the frequent use of repetition throughout the novel. Huxley explicitly stresses the “night-long repetitions” and the “endless repetitions” of hypnopaedic slogans and rhymes such as “Everyone works for everyone else. We can’t do without anyone. Even Epsilons are useful. We couldn’t do without Epsilons. Everyone works for everyone else. We can’t do without anyone” (p. 68). Repetition is predominantly used for emphasis, e.g. when Lenina repeats the words she often uses when she dislikes something: “ODD, ODD, odd” (p. 80). When the Director is confronted with Linda and his son, Linda repeats “I’m Linda!” (p. 132) and the Savage repeats: “My father!” (p. 132) several times until the Director hurries out of the room. In order to prevent the distribution of soma the Savage repeats: “It’s poison” (p. 184) and “You’re free” (p. 186). When his mother is dying, the Savage is reminded of his childhood and wistfully repeats his mother’s lullaby: “A, B, C, vitamin D …” (p. 178). Repetition is also used to express deeply felt grief: “‘Oh, God, God, God …’ The Savage kept repeating to himself. In the chaos of grief and remorse that filled his mind it was the one articulate word. ‘God!’ he whispered it aloud. ‘God …’” (p. 181).
Huxley likes to use and also repeat onomatopoetic sounds or words such as “zip” (pp. 125, 144), “slobber”, “blubber” (p. 106), “slap” (p. 111), “gurgles and twitterings” (p. 22), “drop” (p. 119), “click” (p. 156), “buzz” (p. 129), “dab” (p. 145), “tom-tom” (p. 73), “Thump!” (p. 147) Most of them, in particular the repetition of “zip”, have a comic effect.
Repetition, incomplete sentences (pp. 40 ff, 76), exclamations, enumeration (pp. 40, 152, 173), rhetorical questions (pp. 186 f), montage (pp. 40 ff), telegraphic style (p. 89), etc contribute to a concise and sometimes also dynamic and dramatic style, for instance the repeated “Help!” and “Quick!” (p. 186).
Poetic devices such as rhyme and alliteration are used in hypnopaedic slogans and for emphasis, e.g. “no leisure from pleasure” (p. 53), “walking and talking” (p. 81) and “deer or steer, puma or porcupine” (p. 94).
Huxley likes to use abbreviations and neologisms to underline the technically oriented dystopian society, e.g. “vibro-vac”, “V.P.S.” (Violent Passion Surrogate)

(p. 163), "DHC" (Director of Hatcheries and Conditioning) (p. 15), "Y.M.F.A." (Young Women's Fordian Association) on p. 144 in analogy to Y.M.C. [Christian] A.; "electrocuted" (analogical form of 'executed') (p. 94), "zippicamiknicks" (p. 125), "zippyjamas" (p. 125), "bokanovskify" (p. 128), etc.
Apart from using some film terms such as close-up, slow motion and sound track, some parts of the novel, which are presented in incomplete sentences and an impressionistic style, remind of a film script or shooting script. For example, the novel begins with a kind of establishing shot which allows the camera to pan over the building of the Hatchery and zoom in on the shield of the World State's motto. The montage of various short scenes and statements at the end of the third chapter seems to be a sequence of short film scenes. When Bernard and Lenina fly in a helicopter their bird's view of the landscape corresponds to aerial long shots and high angle shots.
To sum up, Huxley employs various devices to make his novel both entertaining and amusing. But his main concern is to arouse the reader's interest in the serious problems he deals with and challenge him or her to reflect on his warning of a dehumanized future world.

Critical Views of *Brave New World*

In his dystopian novel Huxley does not present a totally perfect dystopia. Moreover, he admits some shortcomings of the novel in his foreword to *Brave New World* he wrote fifteen years later, one year after the end of the Second World War. *Brave New World Revisited* followed in 1958. It is a collection of essays about central topics of his novel such as overpopulation, propaganda and subconscious persuasion as he sees it twenty-seven years after *Brave New World*.

The Brave New World – an imperfect dystopian society

The Director of the Central London Hatchery and Conditioning Centre tells Bernard Marx that "Alphas are so conditioned that they do not *have* to be infantile in their emotional behaviour. But that is all the more reason for their making a special effort to conform. It is their duty to be infantile, even against their inclination." (p. 88) Consequently, Bernard Marx and Helmholtz Watson deviate from the totally conditioned lower-caste people and believe to be individuals. Bernard is by mistake too small and looks like a Gamma-Minus since he got too much alcohol in his blood surrogate when he was an embryo. As he is despised by his colleagues he feels lonely and wishes to be himself instead of a conditioned being. He also continues to criticize "the order of things" (p. 137) and is finally banished to an island by the Controller.

Whereas Bernard is aware of being an individual because of his "physical defect", his only friend Helmholtz is an individual because of "a mental excess" (p. 63). He is considered "a little too able" (p. 63) by his superiors since he is dissatisfied with writing propaganda texts and wishes to become a real poet who has "something" to say though he does not know what it is. Due to a mistake he has got too much oxygen when he was produced and is more intelligent than other Alphas. But when he is able to write an "unorthodox" poem about solitude, he is considered dangerous to the dystopian society and sent to the Falklands by the Controller.
Thus the industrial production of dystopian people is not as perfect as the Director tries to make his students believe at the beginning of the novel though he has to admit that after an earthquake there were "unforeseen wastages" in the Decanting Room (p. 14). Huxley mentions several other defects that occurred during the production process, for instance that George Edzel's ears are too big and Benito Hoover is "too hairy" (p. 55). He thus ridicules the industrialized production of people. When Lenina longs for meeting John, she forgets to vaccinate an embryo against sleeping sickness which several years later causes the death of the young Alpha-Minus (cf. pp. 163f). When the Director meets Linda and his son he is laughed at by the Alpha workers who upset test-tubes of spermatozoa (cf. pp. 131, 132), which is excused by "accidents will happen" (p. 61).
The conditioning of the children is not really perfect because there is the danger of deconditioning, for instance when the Director enthusiastically bangs the table and wakes the children who are sleep-taught or when the Savage mourns for his mother and thus is "undoing all their [the Nurses'] wholesome death-conditioning" of the children (p. 180). But it seems to be Huxley's mistake when he makes the Director mention that there is always the risk that the children could read "something which might undesirably decondition one of their reflexes" (p. 24) since books that are considered dangerous for the stability of the brave new world are prohibited by the Controller and are said not to be available.
Though history is considered "bunk" in the brave new world not only the Controller knows historical facts but also the Director and the Provost at Eton. The Controller underlines that the dystopian people are unable to feel strong passions, but several of them also feel lonely, blush or become furious and aggressive such as the Delta workers when the Savage tries to prevent them from taking soma. As soma is always needed to suppress feelings of sadness and depression, the dystopian people obviously cannot be conditioned to be "happy" whatever happens to them. Lenina for instance is horrified about the life on the Reservation (cf. p. 99) and is sobbing and shuddering after the cruel Indian ceremony (cf. p. 102). "Lenina was left to face the horrors of Malpais unaided" (p. 99), since she forgot to take soma with her. Even Henry Foster, who appears to be fully conditioned, feels melancholy for

a moment when he is reminded of death during his flight over the Crematorium: "It was some human being finally and definitely disappearing. Going up in a squirt of hot gas" (pp. 64f).

Fanny needs a Pregnancy Substitute because fertile women in the brave new world desire to feel pregnant. Moreover, there is still an Abortion Centre in Chelsea (cf. p. 106) though fertile women have to wear Malthusian Belts to prevent pregnancy. Linda for instance becomes pregnant by mistake. It is obviously not possible to eliminate all natural feelings. Even the liftman, the most unintelligent member of the lowest caste, longs for sunshine (cf. pp. 57f). Though everybody is hypnopaedically conditioned to be promiscuous, Lenina and Fanny do not always feel like it (cf. pp. 43f). Huxley does not merely describe Lenina's wish to have sex with the Savage as promiscuous but underlines her strong emotions: She likes John "more than anybody I've ever known" (p. 152) and "I shall always like him" (p. 164). Lenina also likes Bernard though he is too small for an Alpha and despised by others. She frequently expresses emotions such as grief, fear, disgust, horror.

Even the Director, who first appears to be self-controlled, makes a mistake when he is overcome by a strong feeling of enthusiasm (cf. p. 30), is not able to explain why he tells Bernard about the loss of Linda on the Reservation and is haunted by dreams because he feels guilty (cf. p. 88). Obviously it is not possible in the brave new world to control man's sub-consciousness.

The Alpha students at Eton are supposed to "take responsibilities and deal with unexpected emergencies" (p. 141), which means that they are not totally conditioned and that the dystopian society is not as stable as pretended by the Controller. Moreover, police is needed to put down the Savage's revolt against the distribution of soma (cf. pp. 186f), though their use of water pistols has also a comic effect as well as the description of Bernard's bleeding nose. Nevertheless, violence is also necessary in the brave new world contrary to Huxley's concept of non-violence.

It is not possible to juvenate the old people in the brave new world but only to keep them outwardly young looking until they die at sixty.

Several problems of any society are only superficially mentioned by Huxley or even ignored, such as energy production, waste management, environmental protection, etc though he was interested in ecological problems before writing *Brave New World*. The reader could also ask why the Savage is able to read and – to a certain extent – understand Shakespeare's works despite the difficult archaic and poetic language and the manifold demanding themes. Some readers might also raise the question whether the Controller's decision to give up true science for his powerful position is really convincing since he regrets it and knows what true happiness is. Though he gradually runs out of arguments during the discussion with the Savage, he decides to continue his experiment with John without telling why and how. As a Controller he should be aware of the defects of the brave new world

instead of deceiving himself and believing in a dystopian stability that has not been achieved.
In his "Foreword" to the novel written one year after the end of the Second World War and in *Brave New World Revisited* (1958) Huxley does not refer to most of the defects of the dystopian society. But he admits that there are some "faults" and that – most of all – he should have offered the Savage a third alternative apart from living on the Reservation or committing suicide in the brave new world. Moreover, he gives some reasons why he did not rewrite the novel. Instead, he concentrates on the question to what extent his predictions and warnings contained in his dystopian novel have already come true in reality or endanger the future development of mankind.

Huxley's "Foreword" to the novel (1946)

Readers who wish to read *Brave New World* without being influenced by critics and the author's view of his novel and want to form their own opinion, should read Huxley's foreword not before but after having read the novel since Huxley reflects on the so-called shortcomings of his novel "as an older, other person" and against the backdrop of a different time.
In his foreword Huxley gives reasons why he does not rewrite the novel despite its defects. If he did, he "should probably get rid not only of some of the faults of the story, but also of such merits as it originally possessed." Instead, he wants to "think about something else" (p. 224). The ideas he develops in his "Foreword" and also in *Brave New World Revisited* could challenge the reader to discuss to what extent the dystopian novel of 1931 contains "predictions" that have already come true or might come true in the future if such dangerous developments are not stopped in time.
The first "most serious defect in the story" Huxley mentions is that "the Savage is offered only two alternatives, an insane life in Utopia, or the life of a primitive in an Indian village, a life more human in some respects, but in others hardly less queer and abnormal" (p. 225). Huxley admits that as a young man he found this idea "amusing" and "quite possibly true". The same applies to the Savage's rational speech contrary to his upbringing, his self-torture, despair and suicide. If he rewrote the novel now, he would offer him "the possibility of sanity", i.e. a community where economics are decentralized, science and technology are used to serve man and religion is "the conscious and intelligent pursuit of man's Final End, the unitive knowledge of the immanent Tao or Logos" (p. 226). He thus underlines his interest in Eastern religion and mysticism.
As *Brave New World* is a book about the future, Huxley wants to point out whether his prognostications of 1931 have come true in 1946. Though he admits that already in the twenties atomic energy was a topic of discussion, he did not deal with it in his novel because he believed that not physics,

chemistry and engineering but only biology, physiology and psychology could change the quality of life radically. Though nationalistic radicals caused "Bolshevism, Fascism, inflation, depression, Hitler, the Second World War, the ruin of Europe and all but universal famine", he assumes that mankind can learn from history, prevent a nuclear war and use atomic power only industrially (cf. pp. 229 f).

He pessimistically predicts the centralization of power and government control to guarantee economic and social stability. If people feel secure, they will "love their servitude" (p. 232) and feel happy. Huxley believes that "the equivalents of *soma* and hypnopaedia and the scientific caste system – are probably not more than three or four generations away. Nor does the sexual promiscuity of *Brave New World* seem so very distant." (p. 233) According to his view, there are only two alternatives, the destruction of civilization in a nuclear war or "the welfare-tyranny of Utopia" (p. 234).

To sum up, the "Foreword" does not really help to understand Huxley's dystopian novel better but challenges the reader to discuss his political views after the Second World War and the problem to what extent his predictions and prognostications are convincing and might come true.

Brave New World Revisited (1958)

In this collection of essays Huxley deals with central topics he also treated in *Brave New World*. In the foreword he points out that he tries to concentrate on the essentials, which means that he must simplify the complex subject without falsifying it. The chapters "should be read against a background of thoughts about the Hungarian uprising and its repression [by Russian troops in 1956], about the H-bombs, about the cost of what every nation refers to as 'defence', about those endless columns of uniformed boys, white, black, brown, yellow, marching obediently towards the common grave." (p. xxii) Thus Huxley underlines his pacifist position.

"Overpopulation"

Contrary to the time when he wrote *Brave New World*, Huxley feels less optimistic in 1958 since "the prophecies made in 1931 are coming true sooner than I thought they would." Even in western countries "freedom seems to be on the wane" and the "nightmare of total organization" threatens (BNWR, p. 4). Contrary to Orwell's *1984*, governments do not use violence and punishment but non-violent manipulation similar to the methods of control in the brave new world.

As the world population increases too fast to produce enough food and raw materials for them Huxley demands birth control. In his dystopian novel the world population is kept stable since only as many people are produced as have died. The total number of the population of the World State is about

two billions as in 1931 when he wrote the book. Huxley is convinced that "the problem of rapidly increasing numbers in relation to natural resources, to social stability and to the well-being of individuals – this is now the central problem of mankind" (BNWR, p. 9).
Huxley believes that "[o]verpopulation leads to economic insecurity and social unrest. Unrest and insecurity lead to more control by central governments and an increase of their power." (BNWR, p. 13) He predicts totalitarian governments in "underdeveloped countries" that will also affect the highly industrialized democratic countries if they run short of raw materials and would be dragged into wars. "And permanent crisis is what we have to expect in a world in which overpopulation is producing a state of things in which dictatorship under Communist auspices becomes almost inevitable." (BNWR, p. 15)
Huxley predicts that overpopulation "in relation to available resources might well become troublesome by the beginning of the twenty-first century" (BNWR, p. 14), whereas in his dystopian brave new world the number of the population and the natural resources are in balance.
Birth control is possible after the development of the Pill in 1951, which Huxley does not mention. But in poor and developing countries many people cannot afford contraceptives or do not apply them because of cultural reasons. One of the main reasons of population explosion in those countries is poverty and old family traditions.
Though Huxley's view that only about two billion people can be adequately provided for can be doubted, the problem of overpopulation has to be taken seriously. In 2007 the world population is about 6,6 billion people. That means that it has tripled within 75 years after Huxley published his novel. According to a UN report of 2004 about 850 million people worldwide suffered from hunger and malnutrition in 2000–2002.

"Quantity, Quality, Morality"

Whereas in his dystopia the members of the five castes are produced according to their specific functions in society, which requires different physical and mental qualities, "in this second half of the twentieth century we do nothing systematic about our breeding" (BNWR, p. 19). As also "most of the children born with hereditary defects reach maturity and multiply their kind" because of "sanitation, modern pharmacology and social conscience" the physical health and also the average intelligence of the population will deteriorate as Huxley believes. The "progressive contamination of the genetic pool" is "an ethical dilemma" that requires "to find the middle way" to "maintain individual liberty and democratic government" (BNWR, pp. 20 ff).
Huxley raises the question of eugenics without giving a concrete answer though he should have been aware of the horrors of the Nazi ideology that allowed to exterminate people with hereditary defects and thus violated fundamental human rights and ethical values.

"Over-organization"

According to Huxley, "modern technology has led to the concentration of economic and political power, and to the development of a society controlled [...] by Big Business and Big Government" (BNWR, p. 27). The material, intellectual and political progress in Western society undermines "the inner security, happiness, reason and the capacity for love in the individual" and contributes to mental sickness and "despair hidden under a frantic drive for work and so-called pleasure" (ibid.), which reminds of Huxley's description of the people in the brave new word. He warns that the over-organization in politics and economics "transforms men and women into automata, suffocates the creative spirit and abolishes the very possibility of freedom. As usual, the only safe course is in the middle, between the extremes of *laissez-faire* at one end of the scale and of total control at the other." (BNWR, p. 30)
Huxley describes modern city life nearly in the same way as in his dystopian novel: "People are related to one another, not as total personalities, but as the embodiments of economic functions or, when they are not at work, as irresponsible seekers of entertainment. Subjected to this kind of life, individuals tend to feel lonely and insignificant. Their existence ceases to have any point or meaning" (BNWR, p. 31). Whereas Bernard Marx, Helmholtz Watson and the Savage are also characterized like that, most of the dystopian people are conditioned to fully adapt to the dystopian society and its lack of human values. Huxley believes it is obvious "that we are being propelled in the direction of Brave New World. [...] But no less obvious is the fact that we can, if we so desire, refuse to co-operate with the blind forces that are propelling us. For the moment, however, the wish to resist does not seem to be very strong or very widespread" (BNWR, p. 32).
Despite Huxley's pessimism in 1958 there are still many opportunities in democratic countries today to defend the individual's rights against the danger of the predominance of the state. But Huxley seems to be right when he points out that the "basic assumption [...] that the social whole has greater worth and significance than its individual parts" implies the danger of cultural uniformity and the violation of the rights of man (cf. BNWR, pp. 32 f). Also Big Business and economic globalization have become evident and are critically discussed.

"Propaganda in a Democratic Society"

Contrary to the inhabitants in the brave new world people in democratic countries are given the chance to direct their own destinies which is not possible if they are oppressed by a totalitarian government or live in a precarious economic situation. "Liberalism flourishes in an atmosphere of prosperity and declines as declining prosperity makes it necessary for the government to intervene ever more frequently and drastically in the affairs of its subjects." (BNWR, p. 42) Mass media such as the press, radio, cinema and TV are "indispensable to the survival of democracy" (BWNR, p. 46) and are misused for propaganda by dictators as it is done in *Brave New World*. But also in "our Western capitalist democracies – the development of a vast mass communications industry" (BNWR, p. 47) contributes to entertain people with irrelevant distractions. "In *Brave New World* non-stop distractions of the most fascinating nature (the feelies, orgy-porgy, centrifugal bumblepuppy) are deliberately used as instruments of policy, for the purpose of preventing people from paying too much attention to the realities of the social and political situation." (BNWR, pp. 47 f) According to Huxley, people who mainly live "in the irrelevant other worlds of sport and soap opera, of mythology and metaphysical phantasy" (BNWR, p. 48) will hardly be able to resist those who manipulate and control society. Huxley's critical view of the mass media is worth discussing nowadays.

"Propaganda under a Dictatorship"

Like in *Brave New World* the people in Communist China and the Soviet Union are subjected to "highly effective conditioning" through propaganda. Hitler became one of the most successful demagogues because he knew how to manipulate the instincts and emotions of the masses (cf. BNWR, pp. 53 f). He achieved his aims by repeating stereotyped formulas and never admitted that he might be wrong. He did not address the individual who is able to differentiate and is able to think critically but he appealed to the mass hysteria. Opponents were shouted down, attacked or liquidated.

Against the backdrop of such historical nightmares Huxley asks: "In an age of accelerating overpopulation, of accelerating over-organization and ever more efficient means of mass communication, how can we preserve the integrity and re-assert the value of the human individual?" (BNWR, p. 59)

"The Arts of Selling"

Huxley believes that in a free market system advertising is indispensable. But people are also manipulated to buy products because advertising appeals to their unconscious fears, desires and dreams. "We do not buy just a car, we buy prestige." (BNWR, p. 67) Children in particular are highly susceptible to television commercials and are manipulated to buy the products of industry when they grow up and earn money. The methods of advertising are also adopted by political parties, who "merchandize their candidates and issues by the same methods that business has developed to sell goods" (BNWR, p. 73). All that is now needed is money and a candidate who can be coached to look 'sincere.'" (ibid.) Moreover, he must be an entertainer who does not bore his audience and is able to "over-simplify complex issues". "The methods now being used to merchandise the political candidate as though he were a deodorant, positively guarantee the electorate against ever hearing the truth about anything." (BNWR, p. 74) Huxley seems to compare the hypnopaedic conditioning of the dystopian people in the Brave New World to have a throwaway mentality and a strong desire for consumption with the methods of advertising in capitalist societies that subconsciously manipulate the consumers. He also warns of the danger of political propaganda since economic strategies and methods of advertising have been adopted in politics.

"Brainwashing"

Based on the experiments of Ivan Pavlov with dogs, totalitarian regimes have also manipulated individuals under torture or psychological stress to internalize their doctrines. "Under favourable conditions, practically everybody can be converted to practically anything." (BNWR, p. 82) Like in *Brave New World* people might be conditioned in their childhood to fully adapt to a future despotic society where everybody is liquidated or brainwashed.

Huxley's pessimistic view of a future nightmare based on brainwashing can be related to his dystopian novel but also to reality. As brainwashing has been applied in several countries such as China to adapt nonconformist people to the doctrine of the state, Huxleys's warning has to be taken seriously.

"Chemical Persuasion"

Huxley explains the difference between the original soma and the soma used in his dystopian novel. Whereas the soma used by the ancient Aryan invaders of India was a dangerous drug used in religious rites, his fictitious soma does not have any negative side effects. "In small doses it brought a sense of bliss, in larger doses it made you see visions and, if you took three tablets, you would sink in a few minutes into refreshing sleep." (BNWR, p. 90). Huxley considers such a private use of the drug as acceptable and only criticizes its political misuse by the totalitarian government for the total control of the people. "The daily Soma ration was an insurance against personal maladjustment, social unrest and the spread of subversive ideas." (ibid.)

Huxley discusses the more or less dangerous effects of numerous drugs on the human mind and body including alcohol and also refers to the medical use of some of them. He believes that pharmacology, biochemistry and neurology will develop and test new and better substances but: "Like everything else, these discoveries may be used well or badly. They may help the psychiatrist in his battle against mental illness, or they may help the dictator in his battle against freedom. More probably (since science is divinely impartial) they will both enslave and make free, heal and at the same time destroy." (BWNR, pp. 97 f)

Huxley plays down the private use of soma in the brave new world, which he considers an ideal drug with tranquillizing, stimulating hallucinatory effects, though he describes the happiness "that follows the release from anxiety and tension" as "negative happiness" (BNWR, p. 94). Moreover, he forgets to mention that Linda dies because of taking overdoses of soma, which in this chapter he describes as a serious danger of the original soma used by the Aryan invaders.

"Subconscious Persuasion"

Huxley regrets that he did not know anything about the experiments that proved "that people actually see and hear a great deal more than they consciously know they see and hear." (BNWR, p. 102) He would have liked to refer to this "pre-conscious perception" in *Brave New World*, since it has been applied in advertising and might be also used by politicians to manipulate people's decisions without their being aware of being subconsciously influenced. In a commercial or movie for instance suggestions to buy a certain product are inserted for mini seconds while the recipient is not aware of the short flashes of pictures or words. But nevertheless he is induced to buy the product or accept the political propaganda. The effect of such methods of subconscious persuasion can even become stronger if it is directed to people under physical or emotional stress. Thus Huxley warns of similar advertising tricks also used nowadays (cf. e.g. Packard, *The Hidden Persuaders*, 1991, 2007).

"Hypnopaedia"

Huxley gives a short summary of the use and effect of hypnopaedia in *Brave New World* and refers to an experiment with a group of prisoners in California in 1957. The prisoners who had agreed to be "psychological guinea-pigs" (BNWR, p. 113) were sleep-taught to change their moral behaviour. Huxley raises the question whether hypnopaedia should be allowed in a democratic society. Sleep-teaching and hypnosis can successfully be used during light sleep, for instance for therapeutic purposes to cure children of bed wetting and nail biting (cf. BNWR, p. 119). But sleep-teaching and hypnosis could also be misused by businessmen and politicians to exploit "the suggestibility both of individuals and of crowds" (BNWR, p. 123) and must therefore be controlled by law.

"Education for Freedom"

Contrary to *Brave New World* where "socially desirable behaviour was ensured by a double process of genetic manipulation and post-natal conditioning" Huxley insists on the autonomy and freedom of the individual "in the world we live in" (BNWR, pp. 134 f). "Everything that is done within a society is done by individuals." (BNWR, p. 131) Man is not the product of his social environment and not less important than community. Huxley supports his view by giving an example: Shakespeare's plays were not written by Elizabethan England but by a creative individual who made use of the knowledge of his time (cf. BNWR, p. 128).

Huxley demands to "educate ourselves and our children for freedom and self-government", which is primarily an education referring to "the facts of individual diversity and genetic uniqueness and the values of freedom, tolerance and mutual charity" (BNWR, p. 135). Such an education is based on "an education in the proper uses of language" (BNWR, p. 136) to become aware of the misuse of language for propaganda. The most important and "generally acceptable values based upon a solid foundation of facts" are individual freedom, love and intelligence (BNWR, p. 138).

"What Can Be Done?"

In the final chapter of *Brave New World Revisited* Huxley draws a conclusion of what he dealt with in the previous chapters: "We can be educated for freedom – much better educated for it than we are at present" though it is threatened by demographic, social, political, and psychological problems. Three of the most important issues are "social organization for freedom, birth control for freedom, legislation for freedom" (p. 143). He demands that the physical and mental freedom of the individual is protected by law. By referring to the Habeas Corpus Act of 1679 he underlines that a person held in custody must be brought to the court for an examination of his case within a specified period of time. Moreover, the subliminal manipulation of people's minds must be prohibited by law. There should also "be legislation to prevent political candidates not merely from spending more than a certain amount of money on their election campaigns, but also to prevent them from resorting to the kind of anti-rational propaganda that makes nonsense of the whole democratic process." (BNWR, p. 145) Nevertheless, Huxley fears that "under the relentless thrust of accelerating overpopulation and increasing over-organization, and by means of ever more effective methods of mind-manipulation, the democracies will change their nature; the quaint old forms [...] will remain. The underlying substance will be a new kind of non-violent totalitarianism." (BNWR, pp. 145 f)

In *Brave New World* all democratic institutions have been abolished and people are controlled by a cynical despot who believes that "as I make the laws here, I can also break them" (*Brave New World*, p. 190). In *Brave New World Revisited* Huxley expresses his sorrow that in the future democratic institutions could degenerate to a facade of democratic slogans used by a ruling oligarchy to manipulate the people.

Whereas in the dystopian brave new world there is no overpopulation, it is a serious and urgent problem in the real world: "Obviously we must, with all possible speed, reduce the birth rate to the point where it does not exceed the death rate." (BNWR, p. 146) In order to realize birth control the perfect Pill that is also applied by men has to be developed. The use of the Pill must also be allowed by the Catholic Church and distributed in the poor countries (cf. BNWR, pp. 146 f).

To provide for a growing number of people it is necessary to increase food production, to conserve soils and forests, to develop alternative energies that replace the exhaustible nuclear power and fossil fuels, to invent new methods for extracting minerals from ever poorer ores (cf. BNWR, p. 148). But “in any race between human numbers and natural resources, time is against us.” (ibid.)

Referring to the problem of over-organization, Huxley underlines that “the means of production are fast becoming the monopolistic property of Big Business and Big Government” (BNWR, p. 149). He demands “the decentralization of economic power and the wide-spread distribution of property” (BNWR, p. 150). Contrary to *Brave New World* people must be given the opportunity to live and work as self-governing individuals who “co-operate as complete persons, not as the mere embodiments of specialized functions” (BNWR, p. 149).

Huxley reports that according to an opinion poll in the United States, a majority of young people have no faith in democratic institutions and do not seem to value freedom. “But some of us still believe that, without freedom, human beings cannot become fully human and that freedom is therefore supremely valuable. Perhaps the forces that now menace freedom are too strong to be resisted for very long. It is still our duty to do whatever we can to resist them.” (BNWR, p. 154)

Bachardy
Aldous Huxley
August 2nd
1962

3 Fast Facts

Outline 1: Parallels between Huxley's Life and Time and the Ideas, Themes and Motifs of his Novel

Outline 2: Dystopian Principles and Goals

Outline 3: Interrelationship between the Major Characters

Outline 4: An Imperfect Dystopia

Outline 5: Quotations from Shakespeare's Plays Used by John the Savage

Outline 6: Genre, Form, Language and Style

Outline 7: Huxley's Central Topics in his "Foreword" to the Novel and in *Brave New World Revisited*

Outline 1: Parallels between Huxley's Life and Time and the Ideas, Themes and Motifs of his Novel

Huxley's life and time		Ideas, themes and motifs of the novel
Born into a highly educated family – his grandfather Thomas H. Huxley was a great biologist and friend of Charles Darwin – Aldous Huxley had to leave Eton College and could not study medicine because of his near-blindness. He was cured after several operations and was interested in various fields of knowledge, e.g. the progress of science (especially in biology), philosophy, culture, history.	↔	Misuse of science and technology: no natural birth and family life; dystopian people industrially produced in bottles on assembly lines (cf. Henry Ford's car production); Delta and Epsilon embryos multiplied to become stupid identical clones; conditioning by hypnopaedia and slogans to be content with their caste, work, consumption, promiscuity and shallow entertainment, hating books, nature, sports; drug-addiction (soma); no scientific or cultural progress; stereotypical life circle from artificial production to being used for the production of fertilizer after death
Studied English literature (including Shakespeare's works) and philosophy in Oxford	↔	Appreciation of poetry and Shakespeare's works by the Controller Mustapha Mond; John the Savage expresses his emotions and thoughts by quotations from various Shakespearean plays.
Huxley was informed by the novelist D. H. Lawrence about the Indians' life in New Mexico; Bertrand Russell aroused his interest in pacifism.	↔	Primitive and squalid living conditions on the Reservation; cruel religious ceremonies; a Warden prevents the Indians from escaping; in the dystopian world wars are abolished.
Enjoyed travelling in Europe, made a world trip to India (caste system), Japan and USA, disliked New York's skyscrapers, traffic, crowds and the entertainment industry	↔	In the Brave New World permanent traffic of helicopters, rocket-planes, monorail trains; skyscrapers, e.g. Lupton's Tower of Eton College fifty-two storeys high

Dissatisfied with his former writing advertising slogans, Huxley wrote poems, short stories, novels, travelogues and essays.	↔	Helmholtz Watson, dissatisfied with writing propaganda texts and slogans, wishes to become a creative writer.
Strokes of fate: his mother's early death from cancer, his near-blindness, his brother's suicide when he could not marry the girl he loved because of the social conventions of his time	↔	Early death of John's mother from overdoses of soma; eye sickness ("ophthalmia") of an old woman on the Reservation; John's suicide at the end of the novel
The British society divided into three different classes: upper class (aristocracy, wealthy people), middle class (subdivided into upper, middle and lower middle class), working class; rather strict separation of the classes by living standard, education, work and sociolects	↔	Social stratification of five castes: 10% Alphas (intellectual elite), Betas (qualified specialists), Gammas (servants and skilled workers), Deltas (maintenance staff and workmen), Epsilons (unqualified workers)
Constitutional Monarchy, Anglican Church: democracy and Christian religion	↔	Democracy and Christianity abolished and replaced by autocracy and the belief in "Our Ford", instead of the Christian services pseudo-religious assemblies, the Bible forbidden, the Christian Cross replaced by T (cf. Ford's T-model)
Criticism of the intellectual decadence, moral corruption and the desire for amusement during the "Roaring Twenties" of the 20th century; belief in truth, human values and the cultural heritage	↔	Manipulation by sensational media, stupid sex films, synthetic music; no human rights, no historical knowledge or cultural heritage, e.g. St Paul's Cathedral destroyed

Outline 2: Dystopian Principles and Goals

Dystopian Principles and Goals vs. Human Values and Rights

- identity vs. diversity
- community vs. individuality
- autocracy vs. democracy
- industrial production, emotional and mental conditioning vs. "All human beings are born free and equal in dignity and rights" (*Universal Declaration of Human Rights*, Article 1)
- conformity and manipulation by propaganda, slogans and drugs (soma) vs. "Everyone has the right to freedom of opinion and expression" (Article 19)
- belief in Our Ford vs. "Everyone has the right to freedom of thought, conscience and religion" (Article 18)
- stability vs. progress
- dissatisfying working life vs. talent, ambition and creativity
- superficial feelings vs. true emotions
- immortality vs. mortality
- hatred of nature vs. protection of the planet
- the dead used for the production of fertilizer vs. the right to die and be buried in dignity
- shallow entertainment and distraction vs. education and culture

Outline 3: Interrelationship between the Major Characters

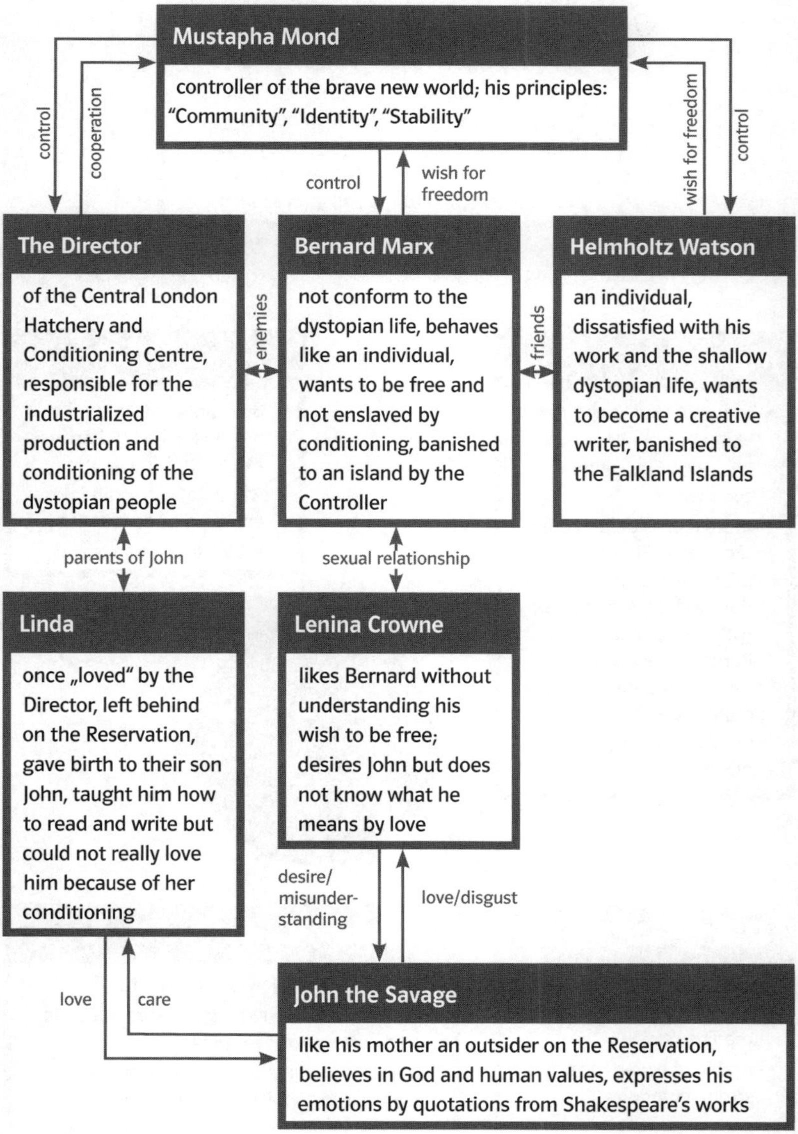

Outline 4: An Imperfect Dystopia

The Brave New World: An Imperfect Dystopia

Mustapha Mond

- believes that he is allowed to break the law
- owns and enjoys reading forbidden books
- interested in scientific progress, but denies his knowledge to the dystopian people
- admires Helmholtz' wish to become a creative writer but considers it a danger to dystopia and banishes him to the Falkland Islands

The Director

- father of Linda's baby John
- haunted by nightmares because of his guilty conscience
- though considered compe-tent and well-instructed, failed his responsibility for the conditioning process which is not perfect, e.g. Bernard Marx is too small for an Alpha because as an embryo he got alcohol into his blood-surrogate by mistake

Bernard Marx

- does not conform to the dystopian life but behaves like an individual
- wants to be free and not enslaved by conditioning
- is banished to an island

Lenina Crowne

- does not change her sex partners as frequently as required by law
- is able to experience strong emotions

Helmholtz Watson

- dislikes the shallow dystopian life
- dissatisfied with writing propaganda texts and hypnopaedic slogans
- wants to become a creative writer and comes into conflict with Authority

Outline 5: Quotations from Shakespeare's Plays Used by John the Savage

Misunderstanding of the dystopian world and its people

- Like Miranda in *The Tempest*, who joyfully exclaims: "O, wonder! / How many goodly creatures are there here! / How beauteous mankind is! O brave new world / That has such people in't!" (V,1,181 ff), when she sees the arriving Italians, John is delighted and quotes these lines when he is looking forward to travelling to dystopia to meet such beautiful people like Lenina (p. 121).
- Whereas John's quotations from *Hamlet* (III,4,91 ff) and *Macbeth* (pp. 115, 116, 119) correspond to his emotions of disgust and loneliness on the Reservation, he first misunderstands Lenina's feelings towards him and misinterprets desire as love. He admires Lenina's beauty and expresses his admiration, love and shyness by quoting from *Troilus and Cressida* and *Romeo and Juliet*. He even sees himself as Romeo and Lenina as Juliet when he reads *Romeo and Juliet* aloud (p. 161).

Insisting on the right of deep emotions and disgusting dystopia

Contrary to the dystopian people John is able to express true and deep emotions:
- empathy with Juliet's grief when her parents intend to force her to marry Paris instead of Romeo (p. 161): "Is there no pity sitting in the clouds, / That sees into the bottom of my grief?" (*Romeo and Juliet* III,5,196 f);
- contempt for Lenina when she tries to seduce him (p. 167 ff): John rebukes her calling her a whore and quoting from various Shakespearean plays, e.g. *Othello, King Lear* and *The Tempest;*
- grief and remorse when his mother died, which is mocked at by "singing words" in the Hospital for the Dying (p. 182) repeating Miranda's words from *The Tempest* ironically used by Huxley;
- hatred when realizing the stupidity of the Deltas and their cry for soma (p. 185) calling them "mewling and puking" babies (*As You Like It* II,7,144);
- contempt for the dystopian people (p. 190) calling them "Goats and monkeys!" (*Othello* IV,1,264);
- indifference towards the high speed of the dystopian rockets, because Ariel, a spirit in *A Midsummer Night's Dream*, is faster (p. 138);
- criticism of Mustapha Mond who defends the replacement of high art by the feelies and the scent organ (p. 191) whereas John believes that they are meaningless: "told by an idiot" (*Macbeth* V,5,26).
- At the end of the novel John expresses his thoughts about God, loneliness, death and suicide (p. 218 ff) by various quotations, e.g. "And all our yesterdays have lighted fools / The way to dusty death" (*Macbeth* V,5,21 f) and "As flies to wanton boys are we to th' gods, / They kill us for their sport" (*King Lear* IV,1,36 f). When he reflects on suicide he uses Hamlet's words "sleep of death" (III,1,66).

Outline 6: Genre, Form, Language and Style

Genre and form

- dystopian novel
- point of view: omniscient third-person narrator, satirist implicitly or explicitly criticizing and ridiculing the abuse of human values
- 18 chapters each of different length which could be subdivided into seven parts regarding the structure of the novel; chapter 15 the turning point and climax of the novel referring to John, the central character of the second part of the novel, chapter 16 and 17 central controversial discussion of the fundamental ideas of the novel

Narrative elements

- description of the dystopian society, the characters and their behaviour
- dialogue, soliloquy (p. 53), direct and indirect speech
- controversial discussion of ideas (cf. chapter 16)
- argumentative versus persuasive forms of discourse (cf. chapter 17)

Choice of words, varieties and levels of language

- predominantly Standard English, but also informal language
- technical language and pseudo-scientific terms
- neologisms, e.g. "taxicopter" (p. 149), "zippyjamas" (p. 125), "saxophone" (p. 70)
- film terms, e.g. close-up, slow motion, sound track
- "baby talk" and words taken from nursery rhymes and lullabies, e.g. "baa-baa black sheep" (p. 23)
- extra verbal communication, e.g. exclamations and shouts
- swear words and offensive expressions
- foreign languages, e.g. Spanish words referring to the Reservation; Zuñi language partly invented (cf. pp. 115, 151)

Stylistic devices

- satire, irony, sarcasm; criticism, e.g. dystopian people ironically named after important scientists, politicians, philosophers, e.g. Darwin Bonaparte, Helmholtz Watson, Bernard Marx; cf. also Pavlovian (p. 21), Our Freud (p. 39), Malthusian (p. 49)
- slogans and perverted sayings, e.g. "Everyone belongs to everyone else" (p. 40), "What man has joined, nature is powerless to put asunder" (p. 23)
- comic effects, e.g. Big Henry instead of Big Ben, the Singery clock (p. 72), police "goggle-eyed and swine- snouted in their gas-masks" (p. 186)
- onomatopoeic words, e.g. "zip, and then zip" (p. 125); parody of songs, e.g. "Hug me till you drug me, honey" (p. 145), the use of rhymes (pp. 75 f., 158, 176)
- John's frequent quotations from Shakespeare's plays
- literary and rhetorical devices: antithesis, contrast (p. 155), paradox (p. 157), hyperbole (p. 64), comparison (p. 51), metaphors (pp. 52 ff. 219 f), repetition (p. 132), incomplete sentences (p. 76), enumeration (pp. 152, 173), rhetorical questions (pp. 186 f), exclamations (p. 186), montage (pp. 40 ff.), telegraphic style (p.89), abbreviations and initials (p. 8)

Outline 7: Huxley's Central Topics in his "Foreword" to the Novel and in *Brave New World Revisited*

"Overpopulation"

- Because of the "rapidly increasing" world population "in relation to natural resources, to social stability and to the well-being of individuals" Huxley considers overpopulation "the central problem of mankind" (BNWR, p. 9) and demands worldwide birth control.
- Whereas there were about 2 billion people at the time when Huxley wrote the dystopian novel there are about 7.5 billion people nowadays. As population growth continues, mainly in Asia and Africa, it is one of the reasons of poverty, malnutrition, starvation, migration, etc.
- Huxley strengthens the necessity of increasing food production, conserving soils and forests, development of alternative energies.

"Over-organization"

- Huxley points out that "modern technology has led to the concentration of economic and political power, and to the development of a society controlled [...] by Big Business and Big Government" (BNWR, p. 27).
- He warns that "the inner security, happiness, reason and the capacity for love in the individual" is undermined and causes "despair hidden under a frantic drive for work and so-called pleasure" (ibid.).
- He demands "the decentralization of economic power and the wide-spread distribution of property" (BNWR, p. 150).

Propaganda, Advertising, Mass Media

- People oppressed by totalitarian governments (historical examples: Communist China, Soviet Union, Nazi Germany), mass media misused for political propaganda.
- Western communications industry contributes to irrelevant entertainment.
- In a free market system advertising is indispensable. But people are also manipulated to buy products because advertising appeals to their unconscious fears, desires and dreams.
- Political parties "'merchandize their candidates and issues by the same methods that business has developed to sell goods'" (BNWR, p. 73), politicians have become "entertainers" who are able to "over-simplify complex issues" (BNWR, p. 74).

"Education for Freedom"

- Huxley insists on the autonomy and freedom of the individual: "Everything that is done within a society is done by individuals." (BNWR, p. 131)
- He demands to "educate ourselves and our children for freedom and self-government", which is primarily an education referring to "the facts of individual diversity and genetic uniqueness and the values of freedom, tolerance and mutual charity" (BNWR, p. 135).
- The importance of strengthening the faith in democracy and its institutions.

War and Peace

- In *Brave New World* war is abolished but not in the real world. There is no peace but a period of "limited and only partially ruinous warfare" ("Foreword", p. 230).
- Huxley optimistically assumes that after the two World Wars mankind can learn from history, prevent a nuclear war and use atomic energy only industrially (cf. "Foreword", pp. 229 f).

4 Impulses and Model Tasks

1. Comprehension

2. Interpreting Different Aspects of the Novel

3. Criticism and Comments

4. Essays, Term Papers and Creative Writing

1. Comprehension

1.1 Aldous Huxley's life and works

Outline Huxley's biography in tabular form and describe the main genres of his works.

Huxley's life

1894	Born on July 26, in Godalming, Surrey, England, into a highly educated family, the grandson of the famous Darwinist Thomas Henry Huxley, his mother a niece of the poet and essayist Matthew Arnold; as a teacher she founded a school; Huxley's father a teacher and writer, his elder brother Julian became a professor of zoology, then director of London Zoo and Director General of UNESCO
1903	Boarding Prep School Hillside
1908	His mother dies of cancer
1908–1911	Eton College which he had to leave because of his near-blindness
1912/13	Study trips to Marburg and Grenoble after improved eyesight
1913–1916	Studies of literature and philosophy at Balliol College, Oxford, finals with distinction; suicide of his brother Trevenen (1914)
1916–1923	Alternative service, meeting famous philosophers and writers such as Bertrand Russell, T.S. Eliot, Virginia Woolf, D.H. Lawrence; teacher at Eton; writer of articles about various topics, literary critic, poet and novelist
1919/20	Marriage to Maria Nys, birth of their only son Matthew
1924–1936	Long journeys in Europe, world trip to India, Japan and the USA; writing several novels, among them *Brave New World* (1932)
1937–1948	Starting to live in New Mexico and Hollywood; friendship with Charlie Chaplin, Greta Garbo and writer of film scripts, essays and novels (*Ape and Essence*, 1948); travelling to Europe
1949–1954	Moving to Los Angeles; publishing essays; travelling to Europe, Egypt, Jerusalem etc; first drug experiments
1955	His wife Maria dies of cancer
1956	Marriage to Laura Archera
1958–1962	Travelling to South America; lecturing in Europe and the USA, visiting professor at several universities, taking part in several international congresses in Brussels, Rome and Stockholm; private audience with Pope John XXIII; essay writing; American and British Academy Awards
1963	Dies of cancer in Los Angeles on November 22
1971	His ashes buried in his parents' grave in Compton, Surrey

The genres of Huxley's works
poems, e.g. *The Defeat of Youth and other Poems* (1918)
short stories, e.g. *Limbo* (1920), *Little Mexican and Other Stories* (1924), *Brief Candles* (1930)
novels, e.g. *Crome Yellow* (1921), *Antic Hay* (1923), *Those Barren Leaves* (1925), *Point Counter Point* (1928), *Brave New World* (1932), *Eyeless in Gaza* (1936), *Ape and Essence* (1948, a dystopian novel), *Island* (1962, a Utopian novel)
travelogues, e.g. *Along the Road* (1925), *Jesting Pilate: The Diary of a Journey* (1926)
essays, e.g. *Proper Studies* (1927), *Do What You Will* (1929), *The Art of Seeing* (1942), *Science, Life and Peace* (1946), *The Doors of Perception* (1954), *Brave New World Revisited* (1958), *Literature and Science* (1962)
plays, e.g. *The World of Light* (1931), *The Gioconda Smile* (1948), *The Genius and the Goddess* (1957, première on the Broadway)
historical biography, e.g. *The Devils of Loudun* (1952)
lectures, e.g. *Lectures at Santa Barbara* (1959)
children's book: *The Crows of Pearblossom* (1967)

1.2 *Brave New World* – a dystopian novel

Define the term dystopia and apply it to *Brave New World* by giving some examples.

Contrary to Utopian novels that present an ideal future world, dystopian novels describe a future nightmare. Thus Huxley confronts the reader in *Brave New World* with a totalitarian society ruled and controlled by one of the ten World Controllers. Some of its predominant elements are

- the industrialized production of people
- their biochemical and educational conditioning
- their hatred of nature and consumption of sports
- no family life and love but promiscuity and pleasure
- the loss of liberty, democracy and the cultural heritage
- Christianity replaced by the adoration of Ford
- drug-addiction (soma)
- use of the dead as fertilizer

1.3 Outline the plot of the novel by also taking into consideration the following points:

- The World State's motto Community, Identity, Stability and the industrial production of embryos as described by the Director of the Central London Hatchery and Conditioning Centre to a group of students
- The infants' post-natal conditioning in the Nursery to hate nature, play sex games and internalize hypnopaedic slogans
- The Controller's explanation of the history of the World State, its principles and achievements such as the abolishment of the family and promiscuity
- Lenina's wish to accompany Bernard Marx, an Alpha-Plus psychologist, to the Savage Reservation, though Bernard is physically deficient
- The Director's story about the loss of his woman Linda on the Reservation twenty years ago and Bernard's and Lenina's meeting her there together with her son John the Savage, who tells them about his upbringing and Shakespeare
- The Director's meeting Linda and his son
- The Savage's friendship with Bernard and Helmholtz, his admiration and rejection of Lenina and his disgust of the brave new world
- Linda's death, the Savage's revolt and arrest together with Bernard and Helmholtz
- The Controller's explanation of his role and the "advantages" of the brave new world
- Bernard's and Helmholtz's banishment and the Savage's retreat to an air-lighthouse in Surrey
- The Savage's attempts to purify himself, the sensation-seeking reporters and masses, the final orgy and his suicide

2. Interpreting Different Aspects of the Novel

2.1 Describe and analyze the main characters and the structure of the novel.

Mustapha Mond

- As he is the Resident World Controller of Western Europe with London as its capital, he is the most powerful man in the brave new world.
- He sees to it that the fundamental principles of the brave new world *Community*, *Identity*, *Stability* are realized.
- Thus he justifies the abolition of family life and strong emotions, Christianity, freedom and democracy, the knowledge of history, philosophy and culture.
- He defends the industrialized production of man and his conditioning to be content with his caste, work, entertainment and soma.
- He owns and enjoys reading forbidden books such as the Bible and Shakespeare's works since he cynically believes that as a Controller he is allowed to break the law.
- Though he once was a gifted scientist and interested in truth, he decided out of "duty" to become a Controller, though he regrets it sometimes to make other people "happy".
- He forbids new research and banishes Bernard and Helmholtz to the islands to secure the stability of the brave new world.
- As a split character he contributes to the loss of freedom and individuality of the dystopian people and also deceives himself.

The Director

- The Director of the Central London Hatchery and Conditioning Centre is in charge of the industrialized production of the dystopian people and their conditioning.
- He is a competent and well-instructed expert who informs the students about his work and feels enthusiastic about it.
- He is ambitious and wants to produce a larger number of identical twins.
- As he left Linda behind on the Reservation when he returned to London, he feels guilty and is haunted by dreams.
- After having told Bernard about that event, he vents his anger on him and threatens to banish him to Iceland.
- When Bernard confronts him with Linda and his son John he feels exposed as a hypocrite and runs off like a coward.

Bernard Marx

- He is an Alpha-Plus psychologist but looks like a Gamma due to a mistake when he was produced.
- That is why he is not really respected and considered ugly by women except Lenina Crowne who likes him and accompanies him to the Reservation.
- He behaves like an individual since he dislikes superficial sex and entertainment, feels lonely and wishes to be free and not enslaved by his conditioning.
- He is revengeful, sometimes boastful and feels important as long as he is John's guardian.
- He behaves like a coward when John is attacked by Delta workers, betrays his friends and despairs when he is banished to an island.

Lenina Crowne

- She is a Beta vaccination worker at the London Hatchery Centre.
- As she is uncommonly pretty, she is the most desirable woman in the brave new world.
- Despite her being conditioned to behave promiscuously, she does not always change her sex partners as frequently as required, likes Bernard despite his physical defect and desires the Savage more than anybody else.
- Because of her conditioning she is unable to understand Bernard's wish to be free.
- She is horrified by what she sees and experiences on the Reservation and can only help herself by hypnopaedic slogans and taking soma.
- Due to her conditioning Lenina is used as a sexual playmate and unable to understand John's love and rejection.

Helmholtz Watson

- Helmholtz is an Alpha-Plus. As an Emotional Engineer he writes propaganda texts and hypnopaedic rhymes and is a lecturer at the Writing Department of the College of Emotional Engineering.
- By mistake he has been produced as an extremely intelligent being and thus feels dissatisfied with his work, sports, women and entertainment.
- Like his friend Bernard he is an individual and feels lonely.
- He wishes to discover his creativity despite his conditioning and write something relevant.
- Helmholtz and the Savage become friends since both like Shakespeare's works though Helmholtz is conditioned not to understand Juliet's grief.
- He comes into conflict with Authority when he distributes a poem about Solitude to his students and also courageously defends the Savage who is attacked by Delta workers.
- Finally he hopes to become a true writer when he chooses to be banished to the Falklands and will meet there other individuals with independent ideas.

John the Savage

- He is the son of the Director and his girl Linda who gave birth to him on the Reservation.
- As he is neither really loved by his mother because of her hypnopaedic conditioning nor fully accepted by the Indians, he is an outsider and feels lonely.
- Nevertheless, his mother teaches him how to write and read without understanding the words in her only book about practical instructions for Beta workers.
- When Popé gives him an edition of Shakespeare's works, he is fascinated by the writer's language and ideas and begins to quote from Shakespeare to express his emotions and try to understand everything.
- He is looking forward to the brave new world but is disappointed and disgusted by what he sees and experiences there.
- He admires Lenina's beauty and misinterprets her sexual desires as love and finally rejects and beats her.
- Contrary to the inhabitants of the World State, the Savage is able to feel strong emotions: He passionately tries to free the Delta workers from their drug-addiction and is deeply disappointed by Helmholtz' inability to understand Juliet's grief and by Bernard's betrayal. When his mother dies, he is overcome with grief and remorse.
- In his discussion with the Controller he rejects the superficial dystopian life but insists on believing in God and human values and claims the right to suffer pain and feel unhappy.
- Finally he decides to retreat to a hermitage and start a new life there. Praying to God to purify him he beats himself with a whip. As he is persecuted by sensation-hungry reporters and the masses including Lenina, he despairs and commits suicide.

Linda

- As John's mother Linda is conditioned to feel ashamed of having a baby, she remains on the Reservation and lives in unhygienic conditions outside the pueblo.
- Due to her promiscuous behaviour she is treated like a prostitute and despised and beaten by the Indian wives.
- As she is unable to mend her clothes, becomes a drunkard and drug-addict together with her lover Popé, she gets fat and ugly.
- Though she is not conditioned to love her son, she teaches him to read and write.
- Because of her looking old and ugly, she is despised by the dystopian people.
- Finally she rarely recognizes John but lives in a dream world of soma. As she is given overdoses of the drug she dies at the age of forty-four.

The stucture of the novel

Whereas Bernard seems to be the protagonist in the first half of the novel, the Savage becomes more important after that. The action of the novel can be subdivided into seven parts:

Chapters I–III:	The production and conditioning of the dystopian people
Chapters IV–V:	The relationships between Foster, Bernard, Lenina and Helmholtz
Chapters VI–IX:	Linda's and John's life on the Reservation
Chapters X–XIII:	John's disgust of the brave new world
Chapters XIV–XV:	Linda's death and John's arrest together with Bernard and Helmholtz
Chapters XVI–XVII:	The discussion with the Controller and Bernard's and Helmholtz' banishment
Chapter XVIII:	John's retreat and suicide

2.2 Describe and analyze the hierarchy and social structure of the dystopian world.

- Our Ford has replaced God as the Supreme Being.
- The World State is ruled by ten Controllers.
- Mustapha Mond is the Controller of the Western World.
- The dystopian society is divided into five castes.
- Alphas represent the intellectual elite.
- Betas are qualified specialists.
- Gammas are servants and skilled workers.
- Deltas belong to the maintenance staff and are workmen.
- Epsilons are illiterates and unqualified workers.

2.3 Describe and analyze one of Huxley's main themes and motifs such as eugenics, conditioning, political control, mass media, the reversal of values, etc.

When you choose one of the predominant topics Huxley treats in his novel, you should also consider what they have in common. They all represent the loss of individual freedom and fundamental human values.

- People are no longer naturally born and grow up in a family but they are artificially produced and manipulated (eugenics).
- Children are not educated but sleep-taught and conditioned.
- The inhabitants of the dystopian world are conditioned to be content with their life and work as long as they live. They are no free citizens living in a democratic society but have to follow the rules of the World Controller.
- The mass media do not inform but entertain their readers or viewers according to their caste-specific conditioning.
- Reading literature such as Shakespeare's works or listening to classical music is replaced by consuming superficial films, stupid songs and synthetic sounds.
- The goal of science is not truth but it is misused to manipulate and deceive people.
- Fundamental human rights and values have been reversed. Instead of God, Our Ford is adored, family relationships are considered obscene, love is replaced by promiscuity, happiness by pleasure, human feelings such as pain and fear by taking the drug soma.

2.4 Describe the photo of Eton College showing Lupton's Tower and the statue of King Henry VI, the founder of the College, and explain Huxley's changes of the place in *Brave New World*, pp. 140 ff.

Eton College

2.5 Principles of education

Describe the teachers, students and the teaching methods applied at Eton College in *Brave New World* (cf. pp. 140–143) and compare your results with the following extracts from Huxley's essay on "Education" (1927) (in: A.H., *Proper Studies*, 1957, pp. 89 ff).

In his essay Huxley underlines the principle of educating a child individually, which means to enable him or her to learn autonomously and in cooperation with other pupils and the teachers. Huxley's concept of individual education is mainly based on the Dalton plan created by Helen Parkhurst in 1919, whose teaching principles are

- to tailor each student's learning programme to his or her needs, interests and abilities,
- to promote independent learning,
- to enhance social skills and responsibility toward others.

Extracts from Huxley's essay on "Education"

"The teacher is careful, when the child appeals to him for advice, not to make things too easy for his pupil; he is not there to 'coach', to hand out lumps of ready-made knowledge, to give recipes for the successful passing of examinations; he is there to show the child to teach himself. He confines his help, wherever possible, to telling the child how and where he can find the information which will solve his difficulties. For this purpose every specialist room is provided with a small but efficient reference library of the subject in question. The children are encouraged to use this library, and are shown how to profit by indices and bibliographies. The result is, that they soon become adept research workers, knowing exactly how to set about finding whatever piece of information they require." (p. 119)

"Under the Dalton scheme every child works at the speed and in the way most suitable to his individual idiosyncrasies. The naturally quick do their work quickly. An exceptional child will get through the year's assignment in eight or nine months. There is no waiting for promotion; as soon as he has finished one year's work he proceeds to the next. Thus a talented English Elementary schoolboy leaving school at fourteen may actually – if he is at a Daltonized school – be doing the work of an average Secondary schoolboy of fifteen and a half or sixteen. In the old schools this talented child would have had to mark time in every class while he waited for the end of the year for his promotion [...].

The slow boy will perhaps take eighteen or even twenty-four months to accomplish a year's work. But he will accomplish it thoroughly, he will have mastered every word. Under the old system he was hurried along uncomprehending at the heels of his quicker classmates. Slow workers are not necessarily stupid, and the examination records of slow children trained under the Dalton Plan are surprisingly good." (pp. 122 f)

"In Daltonized schools children are taught the art of teaching themselves. They learn by their own efforts, and therefore remember what they learn in a way which is impossible to children who accept ready-made knowledge from the teachers, or learn mechanically by dint of mere reception." (p. 124)

2.6 Discuss to what extent Shakespeare's works help the Savage to understand people and cope with life.

As the Savage reads Shakespeare's works on his own without any help, he sometimes uses the many quotations adequately but frequently in a misleading way. He expresses his emotions and thoughts and tries to understand certain situations and events better through Shakespeare's words but also misunderstands the real character or behaviour of the people in the brave new world.

- When he envies the Indian boy's sacrifice of blood, the Savage quotes from *Macbeth* without realizing the difference between the Indian ceremony and the King's murder in Shakespeare's play.
- As he is disgusted by his mother's and Popé's sexual behaviour, he quotes from *Hamlet* and compares them to a pig sty. He also expresses his deeply felt hatred of Popé by Hamlet's words.
- John ridicules the speed of the dystopian rockets since Ariel in *The Tempest* is by far faster.
- When he falls in love with Lenina, the Savage expresses his feelings by quoting Romeo's praise of Juliet's beauty. Whereas that might apply to Lenina who is described as the most beautiful girl in the brave new world, John is misled when he believes that she is innocent and a virgin like Juliet.
- The most frequent quotation from Shakespeare is taken from *The Tempest*, which has also become the title of the novel. When the Savage is looking forward to visiting the world state, he joyfully exclaims: "O brave new world!" and believes that he will meet "beauteous mankind" there. But after his visits to Eton College and to a factory, he is disgusted and uses the quotation full of bitter irony.
- When the Savage broods over death at the end of the novel, he quotes from *Macbeth* and *King Lear* to stress his despair since even Shakespeare does not offer a final answer and comfort.

2.7 Analyze Huxley's language and style by referring for instance to his use of "scientific" terms, names, satire and irony, antithesis and repetition.

- Scientific terms such as ovum, incubator, embryo, etc are used to underline the misuse of science.
- Huxley coins several pseudo-scientific expressions such as bokanovskification and Podsnap's Technique to describe the biochemical manipulation of embryos.
- Terms used in a different sense such as Hatchery, Fertilizer and decant are used to describe the industrialized production of people.
- Technological progress is described by neologisms such as taxicopter and sporticopter.
- The names Huxley gives to dystopian buildings, people, sports, clothes, etc sound more or less ironical, satirical or ridiculous, e.g. Big Henry, Westminster Abbey Cabaret, Mustapha Mond, Darwin Bonaparte, Polly Trotsky, Centrifugal Bumble-puppy, zippijamas, sexophones.
- Huxley likes to use different varieties of English such as baby talk, swear words or extra verbal communication to convey a vivid impression, achieve an onomatopoetic effect or satirize human behaviour. This also applies to the parody of nursery rhymes, lullabies and hymns.

- Antithesis is for instance used to confront the life on the reservation with the dystopian world or stress the argument between the Controller and the Savage.
- Repetition is one of the most frequent devices used by Huxley to underscore the stupidity of the hypnopaedic slogans and the infantile behaviour of the dystopians.
- Comparison and metaphors are employed to convey a graphic impression, e.g. when the sounds of a helicopter are described in a rather onomatopoetic way.
- Symbols such as the sign of the T instead of the cross stress the perversion of religion.

3. Criticism and Comments

3.1 Comment on the principles Community, Identity and Stability of the brave new world and point out why the meaning of the words has been perverted by referring to Huxley's dystopian society.

- The inhabitants of the brave new world are industrially produced and conditioned according to the three fundamental principles.
- They are never alone but are conditioned to live and die as part of the community. Man is defined as a "social" being without any right to live an individual life. Alphas like Bernard and Helmholtz, who are not willing to fully adapt to the community life but feel lonely and wish to be individuals, are banished to an island. Though they are not totally conditioned, they are expected to conform.
- The members of each of the five castes are produced and conditioned in such a way that they are identical beings, i.e. Alphas, Betas, Gammas, Deltas or Epsilons. The lower caste people are identical twins and infantile or even illiterates due to the specific manipulation of their production process. They are content with their life and work and unable to wish anything else. Because of their hypnopaedical conditioning their mind is "the sum of the suggestions" as long as they live (cf. p. 21). As the Alphas Bernard and Helmholtz are not totally conditioned because of mistakes during their production, they are to a certain extent able to behave like individuals and are dissatisfied with their situation.
- Stability is the most important principle of the brave new world because the dystopian society is based on the total manipulation and conditioning of its inhabitants, who are "so conditioned that they practically can't help behaving as they ought to behave. And if anything should go wrong, there's *soma*" (p. 199).
- "Peace" and "safety" have been forced upon the people after the Nine Years' War and are also based on the violent oppression of the Indians.
- Thus the meaning of the words community, identity and stability is perverted, since the dystopian people are not at all able to participate in a community of free individuals. Social stability is not achieved in a democratic way but the result of total manipulation and control.

3.2 The importance of history

Comment on Ford's statement "History is bunk" by giving some historical and current examples. You could also refer to some of Huxley's examples of ancient cultures (cf. p. 35).

3.3 Family life

The Controller refers to Sigmund Freud when he describes "the appalling dangers of family life" (p. 39). Comment on the view of family relationships and the role of families in dystopia (pp. 39 ff) and the present time.

3.4 Aging and the youth cult

Lenina is described as extraordinarily beautiful and admired by everybody including the Savage. Huxley has published an essay about the beauty industry when he was writing *Brave New World* in 1931. Comment on Huxley's view of the "modern cult of beauty" by also referring to Lenina and Fanny Crowne in his novel.

Extract from Huxley's essay "The Beauty Industry"
(in: *Music at Night and Other Essays,* 1960, pp. 228–236)

"[...] What are the practical results of this modern cult of beauty? The exercises and the massage, the health motors and the skin foods – to what have they led? Are women more beautiful than they were? Do they get something for the enormous expenditure of energy, time, and money demanded of them by the beauty-cult? These are questions which it is difficult to answer. For the facts seem to contradict themselves. [...] It is a success in so far as more women retain their youthful appearance to a greater age than in the past. [...] This desirable consummation will be due in part to skin foods and injections of paraffin-wax, facial surgery, mud baths, and paint, in part to improved health [...]. Successful in prolonging the appearance of youth, of realizing or simulating the symptoms of health, the campaign inspired by this cult remains fundamentally a failure. Its operations do not touch the deepest source of beauty – the experiencing soul." (pp. 231 ff)

3.5 An imperfect dystopian world or mistakes of the author?

You could write an essay about the problem to what extent the brave new world is presented as an imperfect society or to what extent you believe that certain incompatible or incomprehensible elements are the author's mistakes, e.g.

- "defective" people such as Bernard and Helmholtz and the danger of "deconditioning",
- the Director's guilty conscience and dreams,
- Lenina's deviation from promiscuity and her strong emotions,
- pregnancy substitutes,
- the Delta workers' aggressiveness when they are not given soma,
- no explanation of several problems such as the provision of sperms, waste management, raw materials, the limits of technical progress, etc.

3.6 Point out to what extent Huxley's "Foreword" helps to understand the novel.

As the "Foreword" was written about 15 years after the novel, Huxley does not want to help the reader understand his novel better but – as an older person – reflect on some shortcomings of his novel against the backdrop of a different time, i.e. after the Second World War.

- Huxley does not want to rewrite the novel despite its defects. He admits that he should have offered a third alternative to the Savage, namely "the possibility of sanity".
- Though atomic energy was a topic of discussion when he wrote his novel, he did not refer to it because he believed that not physics, chemistry and engineering could change the quality of life but only biology, physiology and psychology.
- He assumes that despite the disaster caused by nationalistic radicals like Hitler and Stalin mankind can learn from history, prevent a nuclear war and use atomic energy industrially only.
- But he pessimistically predicts the centralization of power and government control since people who feel economically and socially secure will love the "welfare-tyranny".

3.7 Comment on Huxley's view of his novel in *Brave New World Revisited*, in particular consider the omissions he admits and his predictions referring to overpopulation, eugenics, technological progress, consumption, mass entertainment, etc.

3.8 Comment on Neil Postman's view of Huxley's *Brave New World*, which he presents in his book *Amusing Ourselves to Death. Public Discourse in the Age of Show Business* (1985), pp. 155–163. Also give some historical or current examples of oppression and thought-control.

The Huxleyan Warning

There are two ways by which the spirit of a culture may be shrivelled.
In the first – the Orwellian – culture becomes a prison. In the second – the Huxleyan – culture becomes a burlesque.
No one needs to be reminded that our world is now marred by many prison-cultures whose structure Orwell described accurately in his parables. If one were to read both 1984 and *Animal Farm*, and then for good measure, Arthur Koestler's *Darkness at Noon*, one would have a fairly precise blueprint of the machinery of thought-control as it currently operates in scores of countries and on millions of people. Of course, Orwell was not the first to teach us about the spiritual devastations of tyranny. What is irreplaceable about his work is his insistence that it makes little difference if our wardens are inspired by right- or left-wing ideologies. The gates of the prison are equally impenetrable, surveillance equally rigorous, icon-worship equally pervasive.
What Huxley teaches us is that in the age of advanced technology, spiritual devastation is more likely to come from an enemy with a smiling face than from one whose countenance exudes suspicion and hate. In the Huxleyan prophecy, Big Brother does not watch us, by his choice. We watch him, by ours. There is no need for warders or gates or Ministries of Truth. When a population becomes distracted by trivia, when cultural life is redefined as a perpetual round of entertainments, when serious public conversation becomes a form of baby-talk, when, in short, a people become an audience and their public business a vaudeville act, then a nation finds itself at risk; culture-death is a clear possibility.
[...]
As nowhere else in the world, Americans have moved far and fast in bringing to a close the age of the slow-moving printed word, and having gained to television sovereignty over all of their institutions. By ushering in the Age of

Television, America has given the world the clearest available glimpse of the Huxleyan future.

[...]

For in the end, he [Huxley] was trying to tell us that what afflicted the people in *Brave New World* was not that they were laughing instead of thinking, but that they did not know what they were laughing about and why they had stopped thinking.

3.9 The misuse of language

Describe and comment on some examples of the misuse of language Huxley presents in *Brave New World*.
You could also refer to the following extract from Huxley's essay "Words and Behaviour" (1936), pp. 83–85:

> Inappropriate and badly chosen words vitiate thought and lead to wrong or foolish conduct. Most ignorances are vincible, and in the greater number of cases stupidity is what the Buddha pronounced it to be, a sin. For, consciously or sub-consciously, it is with deliberation that we do not know or fail to understand – because incomprehension allows us, with a good conscience, to evade unpleasant obligations and responsibilities, because ignorance is the best excuse for going on doing what one likes, but ought not, to do.
>
> Now, language is, among other things, a device which men use for suppressing and distorting the truth.
> The most shocking fact about war is that its victims and its instruments are individual human beings, and that these individual human beings are condemned by the monstrous conventions of politics to murder or be murdered in quarrels not their own, to inflict upon the innocent and, innocent themselves of any crime against their enemies, to suffer cruelties of every kind.
> The language of strategy and politics is designed, so far as it is possible, to conceal this fact, to make it appear as though wars were not fought by individuals drilled to murder one another in cold blood and without provocation, but either by impersonal and therefore wholly non-moral and impassible forces, or else by personified abstractions.

If you know George Orwell's *1984*, you could also compare Huxley's view of the misuse of language with Orwell's description of "The Principles of Newspeak" (Orwell, 2008, pp. 312 ff).

4. Essays, Term Papers and Creative Writing

In *Brave New World* Huxley alludes to several biographical and historical facts such as World War I, the "roaring twenties", the Wall Street Crash and the Depression (1929–1934), his interest in pacifism, science and technology, etc. Moreover, Huxley wrote a lot of essays about various themes. Some of them are also dealt with or alluded to in *Brave New World*. The following extracts from some of his essays could inspire you to write an essay or term paper on one of the topics by referring to your own knowledge and experience. You could also make use of the additional materials offered in this study aid and information from the Internet or other sources including the bibliography on pp. 141 f. When writing the essay or term paper you should depart from what Huxley tells the reader about the respective theme in *Brave New World*.

4.1 Facts and fiction – Huxley's use of historical and biographical facts in Brave New World

You could analyze and explain how Huxley uses or alters some of the historical and biographical facts.

4.2 The problem of eugenics and cloning

You could write an essay or term paper about eugenics and cloning by referring to Huxley's novel and your own knowledge you gained for instance in your biology lessons. In addition, you can make use of the following extracts and further information from books, magazines and the Internet. Cloning has also become a topic in several novels and films, e.g. in Ken Follett's novel *The Third Twin* (1996) and its screen adaptation, and in Kazuo Ishiguro's novel *Never Let Me Go* (2005).

Huxley, *Brave New World Revisited*, p. 19

"In the Brave New World of my phantasy, eugenics and dysgenics were practised systematically. In one set of bottles biologically superior ova, fertilized by biologically superior sperm, were given the best possible pre-natal treatment and were finally decanted as Betas, Alphas and even Alpha Pluses. In another, much more numerous set of bottles, biologically inferior ova, fertilized by biologically inferior sperm, were subjected to the Bokanovsky Process (ninety-six identical twins out of a single egg) and treated pre-natally with alcohol and other protein poisons. The creatures finally decanted were almost sub-human; but they were capable of performing unskilled work and, when properly conditioned, detensioned by free and frequent access to the opposite sex, constantly distracted by gratuitous entertainment and reinforced in their good behaviour patterns by daily doses of *soma*, could be counted on to give no trouble to their superiors. [...]"

Robin McKie, "Scientists clone adult sheep. Triumph for UK raises alarm over humans" (*The Observer*, 23 February 1997, https://www.theguardian.com/uk/1997/feb/23/robinmckie.theobserver)
"Scientists have created the first clone of an adult animal. They have taken a cell from a sheep's udder and turned it into a lamb.
The development is a landmark in biological research – and a triumph for UK science, one that should lead to breakthroughs in work on ageing, genetics and medicines.
But cloning is also likely to cause alarm. The technique could be used on humans, drawing parallels with Huxley's *Brave New World* and the film *The Boys from Brazil*, in which clones of Hitler are made.
Human cloning, although now close to reality, would be illegal under the laws governing fertilisation research. No responsible biologist would support such work, say scientists."

4.3 Scientific and technological progress – pros and cons

4.4 Individual freedom and social responsibility

You could also take into consideration the chapters "Education for Freedom" and "What Can Be Done?" of Huxley's collection of essays *Brave New World Revisited* (see the quotations on pp. 96–98 in this study aid).

4.5 Discuss the difference between the principles of the dystopian world and the fundamental human rights. You could depart from the following extract from *Unanimous Declaration of the Thirteen United States of America* (July 4, 1776):

> "We hold these truths to be self-evident, that all men are created equal, that they are endowed by the Creator with certain unalienable Rights, that among these are Life, Liberty and the pursuit of Happiness. That to secure these rights, Governments are instituted among Men, deriving their just powers from the consent of the governed, That whenever any Form of Government becomes destructive of these ends, it is the Right of the People to alter or to abolish it, and to institute new Government, laying its foundation on such principles and organizing its powers in such form, as to them shall seem most likely to effect their Safety and Happiness."
>
> (Quoted from: *America. A Reader*. Ed. by Julia Bey and Herbert Geisen, Stuttgart: Reclam, 2008, p. 68)

You could also refer to the Universal Declaration of Human Rights (1948): http://www.un.org/en/universal-declaration-human-rights/index.html (15 February 2018)

4.6 Mass media – information or distraction? Write an essay, in which you compare Huxley's description of the mass media in *Brave New World* with the present media landscape.

4.7 Compare the fundamental principles of the dystopian societies described by Huxley in *Brave New World* and by Orwell in 1984.

- Huxley: Community, Identity, Stability (p. 7)
- Orwell: "WAR IS PEACE / FREEDOM IS SLAVERY / IGNORANCE IS STRENGTH" (*Nineteen Eighty-Four*, 2008, p. 6)

4.8 Describe and discuss why books, quality papers, historical documents, demanding films, etc are considered dangerous in the brave new world (cf. Chapter Sixteen) by also comparing the following extracts from Orwell's 1984 and Bradbury's *Fahrenheit 451*.

In the totalitarian society of Orwell's *1984* all historical sources are constantly altered and rewritten according to the current policy in the so-called Ministry of Truth to eliminate every possibility to find out anything true about the past. The majority of the population, which consists of 85% of "Proles" or workers, is kept ignorant by the ruling Party:

> "There was a whole chain of separate departments dealing with proletarian literature, music, drama and entertainment generally. Here were produced rubbishy newspapers containing almost nothing except sport, crime and astrology, sensational five-cent novelettes, films oozing with sex, and sentimental songs [...]." (Orwell, 2008, pp. 45 f)

> "By 2050 – earlier, probably – all real knowledge of Oldspeak [Standard English] will have disappeared. The whole literature of the past will have been destroyed. Chaucer, Shakespeare, Milton, Byron – they'll exist only in Newspeak versions [the ideologically correct official language that makes deviating thoughts impossible], not merely changed into something different but actually changed into something contradictory of what they used to be." (Orwell, p. 56)

Bradbury explains the meaning of the title of his dystopian novel *Fahrenheit 451* at the beginning: "the temperature at which book-paper catches fire and burns". In Bradbury's dystopian society books are considered dangerous and burnt as soon as they are found because they endanger people's "happiness":

> "We must all be alike. Not everyone born free and equal, as the Constitution says, but everyone *made* equal. Each man the image of every other; then all are happy, for there are no mountains to make them cower, to judge themselves against. So! A book is a loaded gun in the house next door. Burn it. Take the shot from the weapon. Breach man's mind. Who knows who might be the target of the well-read man?" (Bradbury, 1991, p. 77)

Finally a group of men with "photographic memories" (p. 192) memorize the books before they are burnt together with their houses:

> "*We're* book-burners, too. We read the books and burn them, afraid they'd be found. [...] Always the chance of discovery. Better to keep it in our heads, where no one can see it or suspect it. We are all bits and pieces of history and literature and international law, Byron, Tom Paine, Macchiavelli or Christ, it's here." (pp. 193 f)

4.9 Huxley thought that his predictions about the future society are more substantial than Orwell's nightmare of violence. You could compare the two dystopian novels and write a term paper about Huxley's view.

4.10 Human values

In his diary about his visit to the United States in 1925 Huxley states: "The thing which is happening in America is a revaluation of values, a radical alteration (for the worse) of established standards." (Huxley, *Jesting Pilate*, 1957, pp. 272 f; https://archive.org/stream/jestingpilateint00huxl/jestingpilateint00huxl_djvu.txt, p. 305.)

You could write an essay about Huxley's view of human values by referring to his novel and his criticism of the American way of life in his diary *Jesting Pilate*.

4.11 In a letter of 18 May 1931 Huxley points out that he is writing *Brave New World* "on the horror of the Wellsian Utopia and a revolt against it." Discuss.

Huxley disliked H. G. Wells' Utopia in the novel *Men Like Gods* (1923) because of its idealization of man. If you like to read this novel you could write a term paper, in which you describe and analyze to what extent Huxley adopted or changed Wells' ideas. Finally, you could give your own opinion on the authors' views and the impact of their novels.

4.12 Compare and discuss the different beginnings of various Utopian and dystopian novels. How and to what extent do they arouse the reader's interest?

H. G. Wells, *Men Like Gods* (1923)
Mr. Barnstaple found himself in urgent need of a holiday, and he had no one to go with and nowhere to go. He was overworked. And he was tired of home.

Huxley, *Brave New World* (1932)
A squat grey building of only thirty-four storeys. Over the main entrance the words, CENTRAL LONDON HATCHERY AND CONDITIONING CENTRE, and, in a shield, the World State's motto, COMMUNITY, IDENTITY, STABILITY.

George Orwell, *Nineteen Eighty-Four* (1948)
It was a bright cold day in April, and the clocks were striking thirteen. Winston Smith, his chin nuzzled into his breast in an effort to escape the vile wind, slipped quickly through the glass doors of Victoria Mansions, though not quickly enough to prevent a swirl of gritty dust from entering along with him.

Ray Bradbury, *Fahrenheit 451* (1953)

It was a Pleasure to Burn

It was a special pleasure to see things eaten, to see things blackened and *changed.*

Huxley, *Island* (1962)
"Attention," a voice began to call, and it was as though an oboe had suddenly become articulate. "Attention," it repeated in the same high, nasal monotone. "Attention."

Ernest Callenbach, *Ecotopia* (1975)

Weston's Next Assignment:
Ecotopia

The *Times-Post* is at last able to announce that William Weston, our top international affairs reporter, will spend six weeks in Ecotopia, beginning next week.

4.13 Rewrite the ending of Huxley's novel.

In his "Foreword" to *Brave New World* of 1946 Huxley mentions "the most serious defect in the story" (p. 225). If he were to rewrite the novel, he "would offer the Savage a third alternative" (p. 226) apart from "an insane life in Utopia, or the life of a primitive in an Indian village" (p. 225), namely "the possibility of sanity" (ibid.). Huxley did not rewrite the novel but had already alluded to this alternative in the book when the Savage asks the Controller to accompany his friends Helmholtz and Bernard to the island, which Mustapha Mond refuses (cf. p. 209).

- You could rewrite the end of the novel instead of Huxley and could also make use of his suggestions in the "Foreword" and in the novel (cf. p. 196) when the Controller says that Bernard's "punishment is really a reward. He's being sent to an island. That's to say, he's being sent to a place where he'll meet the most interesting set of men and women to be found anywhere in the world. All the people who, for one reason or another, have got too self-consciously individual to fit into community-life. All the people who aren't satisfied with orthodoxy, who've got independent ideas of their own. Everyone, in a word, who's anyone. I almost envy you [...]."
- You could also write a different ending and describe that the Savage does not commit suicide but continues his contemplative and self-sufficient life in his hermitage. In this case you could consider to what extent the Savage's, Lenina's and the reporters' roles must be altered.
- The third possibility for the Savage could be to return to the Reservation on condition that the Controller decides to stop his "experiment" with the Savage.
- But possibly you would like to find a totally different ending, for instance by describing a revolution of the Savage and the Alphas against the Controller's tyranny.

4.14 The Savage quotes from various Shakespearean plays. If you know one of the plays, e.g. *Macbeth* or *Romeo and Juliet*, you could comment on the Savage's quotations from those plays or write an essay in which you describe your view of the play and some of the difficulties you had to understand it.

4.15 Reading literature – Shakespeare, thrillers or nothing at all?

In an essay you could for instance discuss
- what kind of people like reading books,
- what sort of books are read by whom,
- what other print media are read by whom,
- to what extent TV, movies and the Internet restrain reading.

4.16 Describe and analyze the following cartoon by referring to *Brave New World*.

"Lord, we know what we are, but know not what we may be."

Shakespeare, *Hamlet* IV,5,43 f

4.17 What has become of the title of Huxley's novel?

"Brave new world" has become a phrase or slogan widely used to describe ambivalent scientific and technical developments, social changes, arriving at a foreign country, etc. It is used as a title of newspaper articles, TV productions, names, companies, etc. You could discuss one of the following examples and others you will find on the Internet (cf. e.g. www.imdb.com).

- Headline and beginning of a magazine article:

  "Brave New World. The Chunnel: Is there a light at the end of it? Probably, but the long-awaited train service linking Britain and France still has a lot to prove. As the sleek, hypermodern train approaches the coastline, it begins its almost imperceptible descent. The earthen walls gently rise up in a welcoming embrace. The lush English countryside gradually disappears from view. Then, suddenly … darkness. You've entered the Channel Tunnel. The next light you see, 20 minutes later, will be the sun shining down on the fields and farmhouses of northern France. As you emerge it's tempting to wonder: why didn't somebody think of this before? […]." (*Newsweek*, November 7, 1994, p. 16)

- At the end of the film *Shakespeare in Love* Viola is walking up a vast and empty beach in America. The final sentence of the screenplay, a stage direction, goes: "Dissolve slowly to Viola, walking away up the beach towards her brave new world" (Marc Norman / Tom Stoppard, *Shakespeare in Love*, 2000, p. 154). But possibly the three words are directly taken from Shakespeare's *The Tempest*.

4.18 Huxley satirizes future film productions by describing the feely "Three Weeks in a Helicopter" (pp. 147 ff). You could write a critical essay on similar modern films.

4.19 Think about a new film adaptation.

In Hollywood Huxley wrote several film scripts. Before he went there in 1937, he had already been interested in film production. As his way of writing sometimes reminds of a film script, you could also write a shooting script of one or some scenes presented in *Brave New World* by mainly referring to camerawork but also to sound and lighting.

- The beginning of the novel is similar to the use of a long shot as an establishing shot. The camera could then zoom in on the three slogans.

- Full shots, medium shots and close-ups could be used to show the characters' actions and feelings.
- Discussions could be shown by the use of over-the-shoulder shots and reverse-angle-shots.
- Flights in a helicopter for instance could be shown by aerial panning shots, high-angle and low-angle shots.
- You could also describe the lighting of a scene and the sound track and for instance decide between direct speech and voice-over.
- Possibly you would also like to make use of computer animation and special effects.

4.20 Hidden persuaders

Vance Packard describes the "hidden persuaders" (cf. the title of his famous book *The Hidden Persuaders*, 1991, 2007) that make people unknowingly buy products or vote for a party. You could write an essay about the danger of manipulation by giving several topical examples.

4.21 Comparison with other novels by Huxley

If *Brave New World* has aroused your interest in the author's writing you could also read Huxley's satirical nightmare *Ape and Essence* (1948) or his Utopian novel *Island* (1962) and compare them with *Brave New World*.

Bibliography

Arnold, Heinz: Aldous Huxley, Brave New World. Schöne neue Welt. Stuttgart: Reclam, 2005. (Lektüreschlüssel für Schüler.)

Bradbury, Ray: Fahrenheit 451. Hrsg. von Norbert Köhn. Stuttgart: Reclam, 1991 [u. ö.]. (Fremdsprachentexte.)

Brave New World. Aldous Huxley. New York: Spark Publishing, 2002. (Spark Notes.)

Brave New World: Contexts and Legacies. Ed. by Jonathan Greenberg and Nathan Waddell. London: Springer, 2017.

Callenbach, Ernest: Ecotopia. Hrsg. von Klaus Degering. Stuttgart: Reclam, 1996. (Fremdsprachentexte.)

Engel, Wilson F.: Huxley, *Brave New World* and *Brave New World Revisited*. Toronto: Coles Publishing Company, 1987. (Coles Notes.)

Higgins, Charles / Higgins, Regina: On Huxley's *Brave New World*. New York: Wiley Publishing, 2000. (Cliffs Notes.)

Huxley, Aldous: Brave New World. Annotations by Rudolph Franklin Rau. Stuttgart: Ernst Klett Sprachen, 2007.

– Second Thoughts on *Brave New World* [Foreword] (1946). In: A. H.: *Brave New World*. Material for Further Study. Stuttgart: Ernst Klett Sprachen, 2007, pp. 224–234.

– Brave New World Revisited. London: Vintage Books, 1994. [Quoted as: BNWR.]

– Ape and Essence. London: Vintage, 2008.

– Island. London: Vintage, 2008.

– Jesting Pilate. The Diary of a Journey. London: Chatto & Windus, 1957. Jesting Pilate. An Intellectual Holiday. Westport (Conn.): Greenwood Press, 1974. https://archive.org/stream/jestingpilateint00huxl/jestingpilateint00huxl_djvu.txt

– Proper Studies. The Proper Study of Mankind is Man. London: Chatto & Windus, 1957.

– The Beauty Industry. In: Music at Night and Other Essays including "Vulgarity in Literature". London: Chatto & Windus, 1960, pp. 228–236.

– Words and Behaviour. In: The Olive Tree and Other Essays. London: Chatto & Windus, 1960.

– Letters. Ed. by Grover Smith. London: Chatto & Windus, 1969.

Huxley, Laura: This Timeless Moment. A Personal View of Aldous Huxley. Foreword by Terence McKenna. San Francisco: Mercury House, 1991.

Norman, Marc / Stoppard, Tom: Shakespeare in Love. A Screenplay. Hrsg. von Barbara Puschmann-Nalenz, Stuttgart: Reclam, 2000. (Fremdsprachentexte.)

Orwell, George: Nineteen Eighty-Four. London: Penguin, 2008.

Packard, Vance: The Hidden Persuaders. Second edition. Harmondsworth: Penguin, 1991 / New York: Ig Publishing, 2007.

Postman, Neil: Amusing Ourselves to Death. Public Discourse in the Age of Show Business. Harmondsworth: Penguin, 1986, 2005; https://archive.org/stream/AmusingOurselvesToDeathByNeil203/Amusing%20Ourselves%20to%20Death%20by%20Neil%20-203_djvu.txt

Poziemski, John / Smolka, Dieter (Hrsg.): Genetic Engineering. Frankfurt a. M.: Diesterweg, 1991.

Shakespeare, William: The Oxford Shakespeare: The Complete Works. Ed. by Stanley Wells and Gary Taylor. Second Edition. Oxford: Oxford University Press, 2005.

Trevelyan, George Macaulay: A Shortened History of England. Reprint. Harmondsworth: Penguin, 1988.

Universal Declaration of Human Rights (1948). http://www.un.org/en/universal-declaration-human-rights/index.html

Wells, H. G.: Men Like Gods. Rockwell: Wildside Press, 2009.